MACHINE LEARNING AND ARTIFICIAL INTELLIGENCE

A Comprehensive Guide to Understanding and Implementing ML and AI (2023 Beginner Crash Course)

Carl Dennis

Table of Contents

Machine Learning and Artificial Learning Correlation

These two are readily confused and may lead you to believe they are the same; they are not. Artificial intelligence is a wide notion that refers to intelligent machines. To put it another way, it is the science that underpins intelligent computers. Machine learning, on the other hand, is the technique used to teach computers how to acquire data and learn for themselves.

Machine Learning and Artificial Intelligence systems are two of the most prominent buzzwords in the corporate sector, and they are often used interchangeably. When it comes to comprehending and distinguishing the two, there is a lot of ambiguity. The most often asked questions are: What is Artificial Intelligence? What exactly is Machine Learning? Is there any connection between the two? However, in most firms, marketing ignores the distinctions between sales and advertising.

Machines and artificial intelligence have become an indispensable element of daily life. This is not to say that the two are not well understood.

If you want to deploy and apply ML or AI in your organization, you must first choose which one you want to employ. Although Artificial Intelligence and Machine Learning are connected, they are not the same. Choosing between AL and ML might be the difference between taking your company to the next level.

Artificial intelligence essentially implies that robots can do jobs intelligently. These devices are designed to do a variety of jobs by adapting to varied environments.

Machine Learning is a subset of Artificial Intelligence; the primary distinction is that it is more precise than the conclusive idea. The ML concept is based on the notion of creating machines that do not need continual human supervision. Artificial intelligence is divided into two categories: applied AI and generalized AI. In this scenario, applied AI is more useful since it includes a wide range of programs, including autonomous automobiles, in order to import stock trading systems. On the other hand, since it is difficult to construct, generalized AI is not widely used in practice.

As a result, this sort of AI can handle a variety of jobs in the same manner that a person would. Machine learning has been investigated as a result of distinct discoveries in Artificial Intelligence. As a result, such innovations are unique in helping individuals to manage their responsibilities much more sensibly. The internet was another innovation that contributed to the development of ML. Since then, the internet has enabled enormous data storage. This has never occurred before. Machines may also be used to see data volumes that have not been accessible in a variety of ways throughout the years. This is due to previous storage constraints. As a result, the additional data generated for human processing makes it simpler to complete complicated jobs in shorter time limits.

The concept of machine learning is one subset of artificial intelligence that we should investigate. This will be a useful data analysis approach since it will automate what occurs when we develop an analytical model. Remember how we discussed earlier in data science the necessity for models and algorithms to assist us to go through all of that data and then analyze it? The machine learning process is where we create those models and then put them to work!

As you would expect, many businesses are already using machine learning. Machine learning is used by almost everyone who is incorporating data science into their mix and attempting to analyze all of that information. During this process, machine learning offers them the models they need, models that can assist them to filter through the information and locate the outcomes they require.

This implies that when we can design machine learning algorithms that function effectively with them, the financial industry, government, health care, retail, oil and gas, and transportation will all profit.

Any industry that wants to outperform the competition, offer better customer service, and make smarter choices based on data will be able to benefit from machine learning.

Government organizations, for example, may utilize this kind of procedure and the algorithms that come with machine learning to assist them to deliver more utilities and public safety to individuals around them.

Government agencies will have many different sources of data to sift through in order to get all of the available insights. For example, they might spend some time monitoring and analyzing the data in traffic signal sensors, and then use this to assist them maintain the lights running at the proper times, bringing people to the right spot as efficiently as possible.

Oil and gas are another field that hasn't received much attention in data science but may benefit from machine learning methods. This is particularly crucial when exploring new sources of energy. Machine learning algorithms will be able to evaluate minerals discovered on the earth and estimate how probable it is that the sensor in the refinery would fail. They may simplify the oil distribution process to make it more cost-effective and efficient, among other things. This is undoubtedly an industry that will gain greatly from the use of machine learning.

When it comes to dealing with unsupervised machine learning algorithms, you have a few alternatives. Some of the more common approaches will include clustering, nearest-neighbor mapping, self-organizing maps, and others. These are the sorts of algorithms that come into play when you want to learn more about the outliers in your data collection, display things that are suggested to your consumers based on their prior history, and segment text subjects.

The fourth sort of machine learning on which we may concentrate is reinforcement learning. For individuals who haven't had much time to investigate machine learning and all that it encompasses, reinforcement may behave similarly to what we covered in unsupervised machine learning. While the external appearance may be similar, what happens behind the scenes and what drives this kind of algorithm will be different from what you see with the unsupervised machine-learning algorithms we discussed before.

This kind of algorithm is often seen in gaming, robotics, and navigation. With reinforcement learning, the algorithm will be able to identify, through trial and error, which behaviors from a set of options will offer you the most rewards while posing the fewest dangers.

When we work with reinforcement machine learning, we will discover that three components must be present in order for it to function. We'll begin with the first component of the agent, which is the decision-maker or learner in this process. Then there's the environment, which includes everything with which our previous agent may interact. Finally, we will discuss actions, which will be what our agent is capable of.

What are the distinctions between deep learning, machine learning, and data mining?

 Keeping all of this in mind, let's look at how this procedure differs from some of the other things we've covered in this handbook. This allows us to see more of the desired findings and makes it simpler to accomplish some of the components of data science in the way that we should.

These three subjects all have the same goal: to extract correlations, patterns, and insights that may be used to make business choices. They will all be unique in that they will employ distinct powers and tactics to assist them to achieve their objectives.

 First, let's return to the previous topic of data mining. We might think of data mining as a type of superset of many distinct approaches for extracting useful insights from our data. It may often use some of the algorithms as well as classic statistical approaches used in machine learning. Data mining will use techniques from a variety of fields, the number and kind of which will vary depending on the final aim, to assist in the creation of our data collection and the identification of previously unknown patterns.

When it comes to data mining, there are several approaches to consider. Of course, machine learning is a component of this, but if the data needs assistance from another approach, data mining may provide that as well. Time series analysis, text analytics, machine learning, and statistical algorithms are some of the approaches and domains in which data mining may be used. Data mining may also go a step further by including the science and practice of data processing and storage.

Then we'll move on to machine learning. The key distinction between machine learning and statistical models is that the purpose of machine learning is to grasp some of the structure that is visible in the data. We wish to fit theoretical distributions to data that is previously known.

So, with the concept of statistical models, there will be a theory behind the model that has been verified by mathematical facts so far, but this demands that the data fulfill some fairly strong assumptions as well.

The progress of machine learning is founded on our capacity to utilize computers to explore data for structure, even if we start with no idea what that structure should look like.

The test that we can conduct for a machine learning model is a validation error on fresh data, not a theoretical test that would verify a null hypothesis. Because this kind of learning might be more iterative than others when learning from data, it can be something that we automate rather than having to concentrate on it all of the time. We perform passes over the data until we identify a solid robust pattern to work with.

Finally, we should look at deep learning. Deep learning is a little different from the other two processes, but it is still significant. Some of the activities that we may employ deep learning for, particularly when it comes to pattern recognition, including medical diagnosis, automated translation of a language, and other critical societal and corporate concerns. When it comes to this one, the options are unlimited, which is why it is such a terrific one to spend our time learning about and developing in the future.

While all three of these techniques, from data mining to machine learning to deep learning, are distinct, they may all contribute to our desired outcome. Learning how to blend them and when to bring each one out at the appropriate moment might be the difference between failure and success in our data science attempt.

Essentially, machine learning will be helpful here because it allows us to take a deeper look at the data, we have by using algorithms that can rapidly and effectively uncover the patterns and hidden information that we want within the collection of data. The way this accomplishes its work will frequently rely on the kind of learning you conduct, the information you want to get out of it, and whether or not the data is labeled for this type of procedure.

While data science covers all parts of data collection, analysis, and exploration of what we can do with that knowledge, machine learning will just concentrate on what we need to do to see what is within our set of data.

With a list of algorithms to assist you, you will find it simpler to delve into that data and get the greatest forecasts that you need to make wise judgments that will help your company expand and your bottom-line increase.

Explanation of the Machine Learning Concept

Machine Learning is an Artificial Intelligence branch charged with providing systems with the capacity to autonomously improve and learn from experiences; this is accomplished without the need for explicit programming. The primary goal of ML is to create and enhance computer programs. These algorithms can truly utilize the data they collect to help them learn.

The learning process begins with data observation, i.e., direct teaching or experience, with the goal of identifying data patterns that will aid in future decision-making. The basic goal is to enable computers to learn autonomously and adjust their activities appropriately, without the need for human support or intervention.

Algorithms in ML gain their expertise or understanding via experience. Machine Learning is an application that relies on large amounts of data to remind it of frequent patterns.

Defined Artificial Intelligence

In Artificial Intelligence, learning occurs via the acquisition of information as well as the exploration of ways in which the knowledge might be applied.

The purpose of AI is to achieve optimum solutions by improving success rates. Essentially, Artificial Intelligence is an application in which computers strive to duplicate or mimic tasks done by humans in a better way.

What are the main distinctions between the terms Machine Learning and Artificial Intelligence?

AI stands for Artificial Intelligence; intelligence is defined as the capacity to learn and apply information. ML, on the other hand, stands for Machine Learning and refers to the development of expertise or knowledge.

The goal of artificial intelligence is to increase the odds of success rather than accuracy. Machine Learning strives to improve accuracy but places little emphasis on success.

Artificial intelligence is computer software that performs intelligent activities. system Learning is a straightforward notion in which the system learns from acquired data.

The purpose of Artificial intellect is to stimulate natural intellect so that it can solve complex issues. Machine Learning seeks to learn from data about specific jobs in order to maximize machine performance.

Artificial Intelligence is primarily a decision-making tool, while Machine Learning learns new things from past data.

AI is at the forefront of the creation of systems that replicate human responses to certain situations. Machine Learning is primarily charged with developing algorithms for the primary goal of self-learning.

Artificial Intelligence achieves optimum solutions, while Machine Learning achieves solutions, whether perfect or not.

AI results in wisdom or intelligence. Machine Learning produces knowledge.

Finally, Machine Learning applications can scan text and determine if the author is delivering compliments or raising complaints. These applications can listen to music and predict whether a person would be pleased or unhappy after hearing it. Machine Learning applications in conjunction with neural networks give several options.

Machine Learning draws its learned patterns from the encounters it handles. Artificial Intelligence employs the same experiences in the acquisition of skills or information, as well as the application of that knowledge in dealing with new contexts. Both ML and Ai have several commercial applications that are quite helpful. However, Machine Learning has gotten increasingly involved in tackling important challenges in a variety of industries. The fundamental premise of using Machine Learning software and an Artificial Intelligence system in a company has been found to play critical roles in improving overall performance.

The main problem is that using AI and ML in your organization inherently means that manual people will lose their jobs.

The Evolutionary Period
A Brief Overview of Computer Science

To complete a particular job in the early days of computer science, a computer needed to be given detailed, step-by-step instructions. Initially, these instructions were input into the computer via punch cards that could be read by a computer system. Computers utilize a binary language in which 1 equal yes and 0 equals no. It is feasible to construct full logic streams and store and represent anything using just binary. This encompasses anything from the financial market to your fundamental information such as name, age, and social security number, as well as the pixels that comprise a picture.

An algorithm is a step-by-step technique that computers employ to complete a certain job. As a result, in the early days of computers, algorithms were written in binary.

Early programming techniques were incredibly time-consuming, but computers proved immensely valuable. During WWII, they were employed to decipher secret codes and compute the trajectories of projectile weapons such as artillery. Computers are significantly better at such mundane activities than humans, who are intelligent but incredibly sluggish thinkers. Following the war, computers gained widespread use and penetrated the corporate sphere for the first time.

If programmers had been compelled to constantly write algorithms in binary, the usage of computers would have remained highly restricted. While binary is fantastic for computers, it is difficult for humans to think in binary terms. Even those studying engineering and computer science must train their brains to think in binary terms, therefore higher-level languages were developed to make things simpler.

There are two tiers of higher-level languages that were employed in the early postwar decades of computer science. The basic level is known as assembly language. This is a lower-level language that nonetheless employs a mental process if you can call it that, similar to what a computer would use. It's tough to grasp, and many people find developing big algorithms in assembly code difficult. The steps may include instructing the computer to transfer a piece of data from one memory region to another or instructing it to do the various steps required to multiply two integers together. Assembly language is just somewhat more advanced than binary.

However, programmers started to create high-level languages.

These are languages that use logical structures and flows, as well as instructions tailored to the human mind. Even said, programming in a high-level language is a difficult undertaking that is immensely valuable. This is why individuals with computer science degrees earn a lot of money.

You've undoubtedly heard of some of the numerous high-level languages available today. FORTRAN was the king of high-level languages in the 1950s, and it is still employed in many scientific applications, such as modeling nuclear bomb explosions.

While it is used in applications like that for heritage reasons, it is also utilized because it is an excellent language for conducting computations.

Other computer languages were created and grew more prominent as the twentieth century progressed. Pascal, Ada, C, and C++ were among them. The C++ programming language was an extension of C that introduced the notion of object-oriented programming. Rather than just writing algorithms, object-oriented languages allow programmers to create objects inside their programs that may be acted on or experience "events," elevating the concept of an algorithm as a set of instructions to a higher level.

Later, the emergence of the internet and smartphones led to an explosion of new languages designed expressly for usage in certain settings. For example, objective-c, a C extension used to program iPhones, was created. Swift took its position later on. JavaScript and Java, among many others, have grown in popularity on the internet and Android phones.

The Machine's Evolution

Humans solve problems, and machines are extensions of our natural cognitive processes. When faced with a seemingly insurmountable job, people "put their minds together" to plan and find out a means to do it. Humans have always done things like this. People may have had to find out how to cross a river eon ago. Then, in 1969, mankind worked together to land two men on the moon.

The early human tools were just extensions of our hands and limbs that served as replacements for the large canine teeth and claws that we lacked.

Stone cutters, scrapers, and spear points were among the equipment available. Although their goals were obvious, they were rather innovative. These were the first efforts made to enlarge the human intellect via the use of technology, or tools if you prefer. This was a huge leap since the creator of a tool had to imagine it in their head and then cut something out of a rock that had never existed before. Humans became formidable hunters by employing knives and spears, with the capacity to slash and tear at their prey much superior to anything a lion or bear could manage with their natural defenses.

The intricacy of tool manufacture has increased throughout the millennia. Initially, development was incredibly sluggish. People started building baskets and other gadgets to transport and store necessities such as food and olive oil. They also created plows, which made agricultural planting simpler. For generations, everything remained essentially unchanged, as if humanity had progressed little beyond the stone age yet were still stuck in it. However, as society advanced, so did the instruments it used.

The wheel was created in the ancient world, allowing people to move goods and people far more efficiently. The Romans built highways and eventually, aqueducts to transport water from distant locations. People were quickly building windmills and harnessing the force of water to create the first machines as we know them.

Early machines advanced beyond the use of a basic tool, which required direct human labor application. To conduct labor, the original machines employed basic levers and pulleys, which are devices that distribute and amplify applied forces. Levers, pulleys, wedges, and screws were all devised in ancient Greece and are still widely used today.

Watermills used the power of water to power a variety of basic machinery. The significance of these breakthroughs extends beyond their immediate uses and labor-saving features and pushes the concept of eliminating humans from the task to the forefront. Since the earliest watermills were employed to accomplish pounding or other work, machines have gotten more complex and capable of achieving the intended goal, which is to entirely relieve humans from labor.

The introduction of the steam engine in the late 18th century advanced this process substantially. From then on, it was feasible to create more complex machines that reduced the need for human labor. Despite the Luddites' predictions, this process has grown the world's economy to the point that every machine advancement doubles, triples, and quadruples the number of employment available. People discover new and more engaging things to do as technology advances. Despite the historical evidence, people still dread technology and machine growth as much as the Luddites did, and they continue to warn of a future society in which everyone would be jobless.

Artificial Intelligence's Evolution

While the jump-in idea is bigger, if you can substitute a machine for horses pulling a wagon or a man pounding something, the next point to ponder is whether or not the mind can be replaced as well. That idea was clearly raised by the early computers that cracked the Nazi codes during World War II, and it had been raised in fiction many decades and even centuries before. Fiction authors envisaged artificial entities capable of independent thought. The notion of a thinking machine seems to be the ultimate end game that would arise from a lengthy line of machines increasingly replacing human activities. But was it even possible?

By the 1960s, professional computer scientists had started to explore the area of artificial intelligence. Rather than staying a domain of conjecture and science fiction, it had evolved into a rigorous discipline of computer science that was fast evolving.

Despite decades of study and tremendous advancement, the workings of the human brain remain fairly mysterious. Understanding awareness and how we learn new things continues to push science's boundaries. Despite this, incredible progress in AI has been achieved over the last fifty years, even though the initial promise of the HAL 9000 computer still seems to be years away.

So, in essence, what is artificial intelligence?

The development of computer systems that accomplish activities traditionally performed by humans is referred to as artificial intelligence. A visual perception system is a basic example of artificial intelligence. Of course, this isn't "simple" in the way that a computer system that conducts visual perception is easy in terms of technology or the degree of difficulty required, but a little infant, like animals, has incredibly highly developed visual perception skills. And it's something that occurs almost instinctively.

Other artificially intelligent computer systems include an automatic translation service like Google Translate, a voice recognition system like Siri, and any decision-making system that does what human intellect would accomplish on some level. Chess-playing computer systems have long been considered one of the Holy Grail of artificial intelligence, and when they were as good as or better than many human chess champions, it was seen as a significant achievement since chess is considered a very high-level human function.

Self-driving automobiles are another example of a more complex system that uses artificial intelligence.

Of course, we know from science fiction that the pinnacle of artificial intelligence would be the creation of a robot that looked and acted like a human. As I write this book, the evolution of this seems to be coming to a close. The notion is that these gadgets would benefit individuals, however, it raises a number of difficulties and ethical dilemmas.

What, at its essence, do people do as they travel through life? They get knowledge through their experiences. You gain better at performing things as you learn; in other words, your behavior adapts to accommodate the facts that you have assimilated. You may argue that your actions are algorithms, and the algorithms have altered.

This is the foundation of artificial intelligence. The goal of artificial intelligence is to create robots that can learn from experience and alter their algorithms accordingly.

Artificially intelligent computer systems can spot patterns in data and can be educated by giving them enormous volumes of data.

Learning Machines

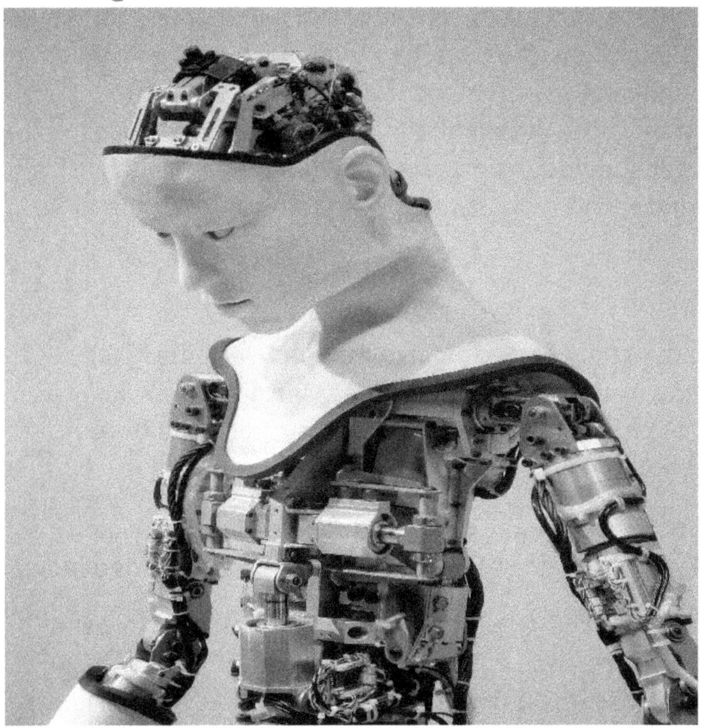

When we examined the growth of computer systems earlier in the book, we said that each step in an algorithm had to be written by a human programmer, and back then, this was done using punch cards to represent the 1's and 0's that the computer would need to carry out the tasks. It is cumbersome to program in this manner, and the computer functions as a passive receptacle, essentially following out the steps that you give it to carry out different jobs and provide pre-determined replies based on set rules.

But what if there was another way to utilize computers?

This is where machine learning enters the picture. Machine learning is a straightforward idea (to explain).

You create a computer system that can learn from data, improve its performance, and make judgments without being expressly programmed to do so. It learns from data by identifying patterns in the data, and it does it automatically, with no human participation required. Statistical modeling may be used to find patterns in data. The more data it encounters, the better it becomes at its job.

This is what "self-learning" entails.

The previously stated algorithms that were designed directly by a human programmer, deciding every single step along the way, demonstrated a radically different approach to computing.

Traditional computer programming involves providing computer orders written by a person or groups of people.

Because machine learning computer systems increase their performance with experience (in the form of being exposed to huge quantities of data), they exhibit certain features of human-like intelligence, at least in a broad sense. Under the hood, though, statistical models are used to spot trends.

In a nutshell, machine learning combines statistical modeling with algorithms. The algorithms will need a huge number of parameters or knobs to be specified. However, rather than being pre-set, they are left free-floating. The method is then subjected to huge test data sets, and the patterns in the data are utilized in conjunction with statistical modeling to determine the value of these parameters. The machine "learns" in this manner. "Training" refers to the process of giving test data to the model in order for it to learn.

In order to forecast the outputs, the algorithmic models search for correlations and patterns in the data. Rather than having a computer programmer do it, the data will configure the structure of the model. The system must be exposed to a significant quantity of data in order to properly detect the underlying connections in the data and utilize that to create future predictions. Remember that in the actual world, outliers may deviate from any predetermined conclusion. To learn effectively enough so that it does not make too many errors, the system must be exposed to enough data so that it can absorb outliers and unexpected outcomes. Of course, the model will not always be 100% correct; even a well-trained model may have missed it.

We may conceive of an example of how machine learning might be used in practice. Consider creating a machine learning model that might be used to approve a loan application. The model would be given data from a huge number of individuals who had previously applied for this sort of loan. The data might comprise demographic, educational, job, and income information, as well as the applicant's payment and credit histories. The algorithm would then analyze the data to see if there were any trends in the data that could be used to forecast whether or not a certain applicant would pay off or fail on a loan.

Obviously, although we may think this to be a simple topic to handle on the surface, the reality is more intricate. To prevent producing incorrect predictions, the system needs additional data.

When it comes to debt, this is an intriguing topic since a person can meet with an application and make a decision on whether or not someone who is unqualified on paper should really obtain a loan based on other considerations.

Those are aspects that, in the conventional sense, a computer system is unlikely to be able to separate.

Assume we built a system using typical programming approaches. This sort of system would accept or refuse a loan based on hard-coded choices placed in place by a human programmer, such as a minimum credit score, income level, and so on. A machine learning model, on the other hand, would not have any of those parameters established and would instead learn from past data. It won't be flawless, but it will help it pluck out examples that provided some variation to the data with individuals who would not be authorized for loans under rigorous guidelines.

However, much like a human banker, a machine learning algorithm may, given enough data, decide to grant a loan to someone who would not be suitable on paper.

Remember that after the algorithm is set up and the data is sent to the computer, there is no human interaction. It may find numerous patterns in data that we are completely unaware of. However, greater data exposure, as well as more testing and training, may help the model improve.

In the Use of Machine Learning and Artificial Intelligence

AI and Machine Learning Projects

Overlooking exaggeration may be tough with cutting-edge powerful technology like the changes provided by ML.

Certainly, billions of dollars are being spent on ML projects. Machine learning is the core of all digital transformation strategies. Of course, when people speak about machine learning, they are referring to AI, either directly or indirectly. As a result, it is vital to have an understanding of how ML works in reality across diverse firms throughout the world.

Because of AI's capabilities, computer machines can now examine large datasets in order to reach a "reasoned" judgment on the issue under consideration. As a result, the human decision-making process is active, with improved results.

Despite the fact that ML and AI are simple concepts, their everyday implementation has proven a huge difficulty. Content matching and recommendations for streaming media is one area that has seen success, and as a result, the on-demand viewing experience is being fundamentally revolutionized. Rather than limiting the "expert" human labor required to categorize, curate, and split the material into digestible sorts, machine learning is the analytical tool in tailored content distribution in this day and age. Following a study of preferences and user behavior, different streaming services may properly tailor suggestions, and targeted material can also be heavily pushed for engagement and revenue objectives.

In general, every sector should include AI in its business models. It is not required to have a massive corporate structure to offer AI-enabled services for improved customer care. AI has the potential to assist both small and medium-sized organizations.

Furthermore, in addition to improving the collection and payment procedures, inventory systems must be altered via prompt dispatch and delivery of quality goods. Additionally, inventory errors and shipping-related concerns should be actively considered.

Pharmaceuticals and Life Sciences

When there is a debate on death, everyone comes to the conclusion that aging is a perplexing experience. Though you don't expect eternity or endurance, you may realize that your quality of life suffers as a consequence of an accident, increasing joint discomfort, or disease exposure.

Deep learning, on the other hand, may delay the aging process. Currently, technology is being utilized to detect biomarkers associated with aging. A simple blood test may sometimes reveal body components suggestive of wear and tear, and your doctor may be able to reverse the consequences by using medication and lifestyle modifications.

Food

Fresh vegetable and fruit sales account for roughly 40% of a grocer's income. As a result, believing in the ability to critically maintain product quality is equal to irony. However, making comments is usually easier than doing the action. Consumer uncertainty and supply chains are mostly determined by grocer dynamics. It might be a dangerous balancing act to keep their items fresh and aisles supplied.

Machine learning, on the other hand, has been discovered to be the secret to smarter and fresher food. In this aspect, ML algorithms may be kept up to date using historical datasets, time tracking, and promotional data. Following that, the data scientists do an analysis to determine how much of each product should be ordered and presented. Furthermore, ML systems gather and preserve data regarding weather forecasts, public holidays, and other important events. Following that, a suggested order is provided after 24 hours to allow grocers to precisely line up their items in stock.

Out-of-stock rates are reduced by up to 80% in firms that use ML in their processes, and gross margins are increased by 9%.

Entertainment and media

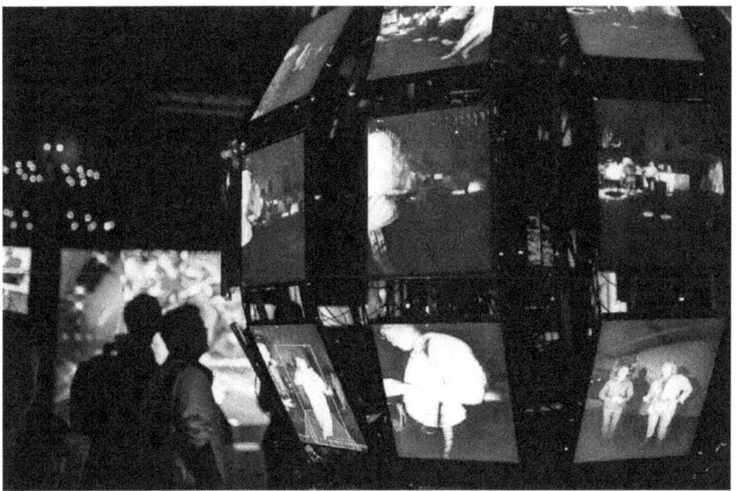

Content from media outlets may now be accessed thanks to ML. Deaf and hard-of-hearing Americans may now see YouTube videos thanks to an automated captioning scheme powered by ML technology.

IT stands for information technology.

While machine learning generates multiple business views, many firms are unable to apply AI technology. However, there are expected to be about 2.7 million data science jobs by 2020.

Law

Deep learning systems are critical in the legal business. Although the legal terminology might be difficult to interpret, deep learning computers can review over ten thousand papers.

Previously, while examining contract conditions affecting their client's company, legal experts had to manually scrutinize piles of paperwork. Contract clauses may now be combined with a computer program, resulting in a faster reaction time and the detection of essential phrases for further review.

Insurance

Aside from countersigning and validating the specifics, everyone strives to reduce the risks. As a result, the insurance business stands to profit greatly from machine learning. Customer data and real-time data may be utilized by machine learning algorithms to assess risk.

The algorithms may also modify prices based on information, resulting in savings for both individuals and insurance firms.

We can convert this process, in which isolated social network data is acquired by ML systems to generate an accurate profile, via a holistic analysis. The insurance sector, in conjunction with AI, may designate policyholders who are in excellent health.

A person who is responsible for those aspects of their life is also a responsible driver.

Education

Students may now learn via Intelligent Tutoring Systems (ITS). These AI platforms act as virtual instructors in this context, and their digital teachings are tailored to each child's strengths. Every time a student completes a quiz, the data is examined by ML software in order to customize subsequent content.

Furthermore, the Intelligent Tutoring System guarantees that students have a lot of information and overcome learning challenges by "learning" the specific demands of a user and picking the sort of lessons that are beneficial to them. According to the conclusions of a research study, pupils who utilize intelligent tutoring systems outperform their peers who learn via group teaching.

Medical Care

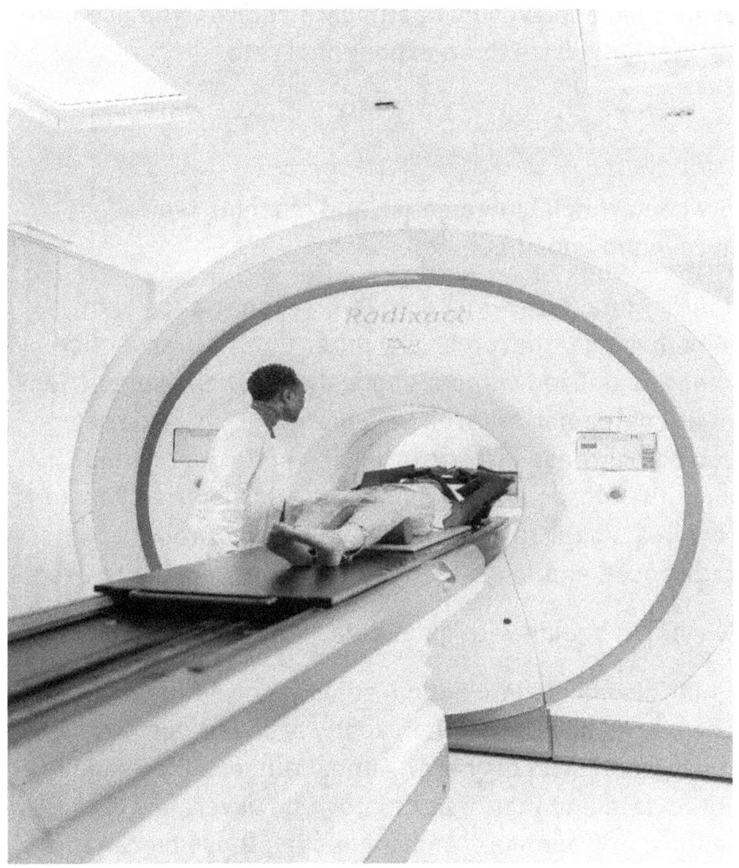

According to reports, the United States spends more per person on health care than other nations. The UK, for example, spends around ($3,749) per person per year on health care, which is less than that of the US. It is sad that, despite considerable investment, health results in the United States remain unsatisfactory.

With the creation of AI, healthcare expenditures in the United States may be decreased, since the number of tests can be reduced and the proper judgments can be made with effective lifesaving outcomes.

Because of the high costs of health care and the advantages achieved by health care choices, the use of AI is projected to rise at an exponential rate.

How Are AI and Machine Learning Improving Customer Experience?

How can artificial intelligence and machine learning improve the consumer experience?

ML and AI have shown a substantial association with online buying. Amazon or any other purchasing service cannot be utilized without suggestions. These suggestions are often deemed tailored based on your characteristics such as purchase history, browsing history, and much more. The aforementioned online platforms are likely to provide a digital salesman who is aware of your preferences and may steer you to things you like to use.

Everything begins with good data.

To put this choice into action, some heavy lifting must be done on the back end. Who exactly are your customers? Do you know who they are? Almost all consumers leave a trail of data and their track history; however, this data is in the form of fragments, and connecting those pieces is a difficult operation. What is the best technique to find a customer's many accounts?

Can you connect a client's personal and professional accounts if he has different accounts? And, if a corporation employs many names, how can the one entity responsible for them be identified? Aside from understanding their alliance, client experience is all about your solid relationship with them.

Entity resolution is the process of removing duplicate entries from a customer list. It is used by big-scale enterprises that manage huge data teams. The democratization of entity resolution is now taking place. Small to medium-sized businesses need entity resolution services due to a lack of startups.

After you've successfully identified your consumers, the following stage is to build a solid connection with them. Gaining a basic understanding of your client's activities is the key to conquering their wants. What kind of information do you have on them, and how will it be used? The data-gathering process is used to build technologies such as AI and ML. When it comes to calculating data streams originating from sponsors, numerous applications, and many other sources, this procedure may be distressing and morally controversial. When collecting data about your consumers, always get their permission and verify that their sensitive information is not compromised.

ML is quite comparable to any other kind of computing: the concept "garbage in, garbage out" still applies in the ML domain. Because of the poor quality of the training data, the outcomes will be degraded.

The number of data fields and variables available changes as the number of data sources increases. There is also the possibility of inaccuracies, such as transcription errors, typographic problems, and so on. Manually cleaning and fixing data is often possible; nevertheless, it is a time-consuming and error-prone operation for many data scientists. The study subjects include current data repair and data quality, which are designed for entity solutions. Furthermore, a new set of machine learning techniques for automatic data cleansing is developing in this day and age.

When discussing the uses of ML and AI in relation to customer experience, the usual area is in customization systems and recommendation systems.

In this current age, well-known technologies such as hybrid recommender systems applications that incorporate several recommender approaches are being observed. Most hybrid recommenders need several sources, and these systems are combined with deep learning models and vast volumes of data. Personalization technologies and advanced recommendations would be in real-time, while suggestions should include models that are simply reoriented on a regular basis. The recommendation systems may be developed by conducting reinforcement learning, online learning, and bandit algorithms on a regular basis and training the models against live data.

Aside from improving consumer interactions, machine learning and AI-based models are improving a variety of business processes and procedures. Chatbots are an excellent example in this instance.

Chatbots are not currently in use. Nonetheless, if developed properly, bots may provide outstanding client acquisition rates. However, we are still in the early stages of natural language processing and interpretation, and several revolutions have occurred recently. Chatbots have evolved beyond providing alerts to handling basic question-and-answer situations as complicated language models have evolved.

Chatbots are predicted to become a critical component for smart and efficient service delivery to humans as a result of this revolutionary transformation. To achieve this level of performance, real-time suggestions and personalization will be merged with chatbots. These bots will need to be able to tell the difference between people and clients.

Machine learning is also being used in domains such as fraud detection. With the rapid rise in worries, there is always an ongoing war between thieves and the correct people when it comes to fraud detection. The fraudsters use sophisticated processes for internet crime. Person-to-person fraud is a thing of the past: it is now designed to act like a bot, purchasing all tickets to an event so touts may resell them. As shown in recent elections, hackers may easily get access to social media using a bot, where discussions are filled with artificial responses. Identifying and stopping such bots in real-time is a time-consuming operation. This is a job that machine learning can handle. Even so, it would be a difficult task. Nonetheless, its answer is redesigning an online environment in which people believe they are valued and protected.

The advancement of emotion detection and voice technology will significantly minimize friction in automated customer interactions. Appropriately responding to clients will become easier thanks to multi-modal models that incorporate diverse inputs. As a result, users will be able to convey their wants, including live-streaming videos.

While people envision themselves in a terrifying "mysterious valley" as a result of interactions between humans and robots, robots will make future customers happier than we are now.

Recognizing the worth of clients is vital if the uncanny valley panorama is utilized to study them. All AI and ML applications engaging with clients must safeguard their confidentiality, and the apps must be objective and secure. They may include some complications; nonetheless, customer experience will not be improved if clients feel abandoned. A more resourceful conclusion is possible, but it is not a good compromise.

How can artificial intelligence and machine learning improve the consumer experience? Many new developments are yet to come as a result of these technologies. Furthermore, AI will now be employed to provide a seamless consumer experience.

Self-Driving Vehicles

What exactly are autonomous vehicles?

To tear down a self-driving automobile, we must first grasp what it means to be autonomous. The term itself is made up of two Greek phrases. The initial phrase, auto, means "I" in Latin. The second term, nomous, is Greek for customary or legal.

As a result, it is easy to assume that the word literally means self-law or self-custom. It has little significance on its own. It is only when applied to an organism capable of thinking that autonomy has a function.

As a person, you most likely have a job or obligations that you handle on your own. When you determine what you need to accomplish, you are independent. The capacity to set rules for oneself and observe them is referred to as autonomy. This implies that anytime you do a given work, the manner in which you perform that task is a practice of giving yourself laws.

As a result, an autonomous vehicle is one that can assign rules without the need for human intervention. For example, if you were driving a car with no brakes, would you strike one person or ten people? This is a typical moral dilemma, and it appropriately concerns automobiles and whether they are a good concept for autonomy. Most people assume that if left to its own devices, the car will just choose the one human based on quantity. Those who believe robots will take over the world in the future have a clear choice: ten humans. However, knowing that it may strike a human, the computer might choose an alternative that was presumably irrelevant to you at the time I introduced this morality question. The machine would just crash on purpose, maybe injuring but not killing the driver.

The moral dilemma frequently includes trains and the inability to make such an extra decision in such a circumstance. However, in the real world, such an issue is unlikely to arise. The capacity to notice another alternative and act on it without assuming the options it will have enables a vehicle to be autonomous.

We, as humans, are used to believing that there are just two alternatives, but the automobile sees more. As a result, if we were given the option, lives would be lost needlessly. This is the most autonomous phase for machines, enabling them to pick the optimal solution without human intervention.

Variables in Automobiles

Choices, on the other hand, are dependent on variables, and if we have an autonomous car, that autonomous vehicle must have variables.

The first variable is the road itself, that is, whether it is straight, an intersection, or curved. Humans would respond differently to each of the three kinds of roads, implying that the form of the road is ultimately the first variable that an autonomous car must cope with.

It must deal with the road as well as the driving rules of the state, nation, or province in which the automobile is located, which includes the speed limit. This is done to guarantee that the autonomous automobile adheres to human-made regulations that safeguard human safety, which is the purpose of training a vehicle on the road. An autonomous car will always be able to go straight since only one variable is impacted. Extra variables are only introduced when the necessity for safety is introduced.

As a result, in addition to knowing the speed limit, the autonomous vehicle must now be able to sight. The vehicle must be able to see such that persons walking in front of it will trigger it to stop. However, humans do not perceive in the same way that computers do. There is a terrific library called Open Vision that enables a computer to detect crucial visual components. If a bipedal form crosses the computer's gaze, it will detect that there are people. This would enable the automobile to respond in less than the time it takes to detect the bipedal form.

The weather is the last variable that automobiles need in order to be autonomous, but this can be accomplished through the Internet, right?

Actually, not if you want it to be completely independent. Even in nations where the internet seems to be almost everywhere, there are locations on the planet where people do not have access to it. In such instances, you don't want an autonomous car driving through the rain if it isn't aware of the weather. Humans behave differently in the rain because they must be more cautious due to their restricted eyesight, which, by the way, the computer will have about the same amount of with a few exceptions. Humans, for example, cannot see infrared, but computers just have a lens switch.

Humans lack the ability to see in the dark, whereas cameras do. This enables the Open Vision system to see in circumstances where humans would struggle.

A Brilliant Combination

Overall, in order to construct an autonomous car, a mix of incredibly creative ideas is required. Because the car must be spatially aware, proximity sensors must be installed within the vehicle. To avoid killing anybody, the vehicle must be able to detect humanoid forms as it drives. The car must be able to recognize the weather it is traveling in so that it can drive accordingly, which means it must have weather forecasting built in. These are diverse industries working together to make it feasible for an automobile to drive itself, which is one of the greatest scientific accomplishments ever accomplished.

Common Concerns

Transport Driver Replacement

When it comes to autonomous cars, the biggest concern is job replacement. The difficulty with achieving breakthroughs in science and society, in general, is that there will always be a loser. As of today, many people are concerned that certain Uber drivers may be replaced by these robots since Uber would no longer have to pay for humans to drive around. This is a similar argument to when Uber first appeared and taxi drivers were concerned about being replaced.

Many individuals are unaware that many others are skeptical, which suggests that this new technology will not be extensively adopted. It will be decades before any of us trust it as much as we trust the Windows operating system. Remember that many of us still distrust the Windows operating system.

As a result, no, it will not replace Transport drivers, but it will enhance their availability. I, for one, would welcome the ability to drive to sites for pennies. At the very least, I know that an autonomous vehicle will not mug or rob me; this is not to imply that an Uber driver would not, but the chance is nil with the autonomous vehicle and unknown with the Uber driver. It would provide those who use Uber as a cheap way to get about town an even cheaper choice, and the Uber driver would then become a premium experience. As a result, when autonomous cars become available, Uber payments will increase since the human aspect will be valued more by clients who desire that human element.

Unattributable Death

When it comes to autonomy and automobiles, the secondary concern is who will be responsible for the fatality. As of today, a few corporations have caused mishaps that have resulted in the loss of life and injuries in other situations. In some situations, the corporation that placed the car on the road was sued, and the story ended there. The fact is that this is exactly what would happen with self-driving cars.

The issue that seems to be disturbing people is that if someone owns an autonomous car, that individual is liable. However, if the vehicle is intended to be driven autonomously, the manufacturer is to blame since they were the ones who mistakenly left something out, resulting in the mishap. Now, there is a good chance that the firm would shift responsibility to the user since the user is expected to pay attention and guarantee that the car is driving, but this would render the vehicle useless in the eyes of many people. When most people conceive of autonomous automobiles, they see what they see in movies, where humans don't bother learning how to drive. They just summon their car and go to another spot.

Companies, on the other hand, do not want to incur risk in their automobiles and will likely regard autonomy in the same manner that they did cruise control. Cruise control helps you to maintain a set speed, but you are still responsible for what happens inside and outside of your automobile as it relates to it. Companies will likely promote autonomy as a function similar to cruise control, in which you will still be responsible for keeping an eye on the equipment. This guarantees that the driver of that car is still liable for any deaths caused by that vehicle since it is a feature and should not be depended on 100% of the time. It's a pretty smart strategy for the firm to avoid accountability when its software fails.

Incidents involving Google Maps

The fourth and least prevalent concern is that the automobile would behave similarly to accidents that have occurred in the past with mapping services. I suggested Google Maps since it is one of the most widely used tools for navigating cities and nations. However, there have been times when Google Maps has been inaccurate. For example, if you have a private community, Google Maps is not permitted to capture images of what is within that community. Many individuals who move into a private community for the first time find themselves needing to give delivery drivers information on how to traverse the area since Google Maps is not permitted.

However, Google Maps might take you in the incorrect way. For example, Pokemon Go experienced multiple incidents with its program because individuals just didn't pay attention to the outside environment while exercising. Many individuals were injured or killed as a result of this since the maps themselves were flat and did not display anything to be concerned about. This was, of course, the responsibility of the individual who didn't glance up from their phone, but the folks were still furious that this happened. People blame the firm, whereas the true culprit was the person who failed to look up. This is the one dread that does not have a quick answer, and it is only because people feel upset when informed they must bear responsibility for it.

The Advantages of Autonomous Vehicles

There will be no more drunk driving.

The advantage of having an autonomous car is that you no longer have to depend on the person inside. Many fatalities and accidents are caused by people inside vehicles who are not completely aware of them.

While the person inside the car may be inebriated, an autonomous vehicle would be able to take that person home without putting anybody in danger to the same degree as the one who is inebriated. This implies that drunk driving-related fatalities and accidents would be significantly reduced.

Improving Traffic Incidents

Several road accidents are often caused by persons being unaware of their surroundings. For example, a person can only see so far outside a car, and many businesses mistakenly prefer to place objects in front of their shop which makes driving more difficult. Instead of seeing turning left or right from the front of the vehicle, which is the safest manner, the person is normally in the middle of the automobile. Small occurrences like these may be avoided with an autonomous vehicle since every inch of the vehicle could be laden with sensors and cameras that would enable it to respond to its surroundings.

All Laws are Recognized by the Software

Furthermore, a lot of accidents, citations, and prison time are caused by a lack of understanding of the law that humans are meant to obey. For example, although everyone is aware that jaywalking is legally criminal, it is seldom enforced. In fact, if it weren't for jaywalking, automobiles designed for autonomy would not generally have to deal with situations in which they may strike a person.

Taxi for Less/Government Taxi

I spoke extensively about Uber and how the autonomous version of Uber will result in a lower-paying tier of Uber drivers. However, this might also imply that, instead of providing a bus for localized transit in Big City, the government could instead offer car-driven Uber-like drivers. Individuals who need to arrive to work on time would benefit greatly from this since they would be able to depend on the government service that drove them to work. This would have a broad impact on many individuals, but it might also have some consequences.

Cars are available for the severely disabled.

This vehicle might drive for those who are blind, deaf, or have physical issues with their arms or limbs. Many people, if they are handicapped, have their ability to drive revoked, making their lives substantially more difficult if they need to travel long distances. Autonomous cars might effectively offer those handicapped people a means to possess a vehicle and normalize their lives after whatever they've been through.

What effect will it have on traffic?

There will be no more traffic jams.

This one truly only applies if practically all of the cars on the road are self-driving. This is something that can be seen in many science fiction films and books where autos can regulate how traffic moves. Given enough data and maybe a network link to the power grid, you might theoretically build a system in which no traffic ever needs to halt. This is because the primary reason for traffic pauses is that people need time to allow other humans to get where they need to go. automobiles, on the other hand, have the potential to create a system in which no automobiles ever need to stop. It would be different from how we now perceive traffic since it would be entirely automated. However, in the early stages of this automation, we would likely witness a lot less traffic congestion caused by accidents or cases where the police pulled someone over.

Fewer Deaths

As I previously said, with drunk driving and the capacity to be a driving law book, there would be many fewer deaths as a result of traffic difficulties. This is mostly due to the fact that people respond slower than robots, resulting in more lives saved in emergency circumstances. Furthermore, most automobiles would come to a stop if they went through a red light before it turned green.

The Impact of Robots on Our Lives

When it comes to AI mental images, robots are a popular choice.

Although they are now limited to industrial and military uses, there is little question that the introduction of drones, self-driving automobiles, and personal robots will bring about significant changes in the world.

Robotics is an interdisciplinary discipline that studies the physics of moving devices as well as the underlying sensors and circuits (electrical engineering). From the standpoint of computer science and artificial intelligence, robotics primarily comprises movement planning: how to maneuver a robot from point A to point B using whatever set of wheels and limbs it has at its disposal. Assume that we have a single-point robot that can go anywhere in two dimensions on a fixed map. Its purpose is to go from start to end without encountering any barriers.

Any toddler can answer this issue by hand, but how to effectively express the solution in a computer program is not evident. There are other techniques, but sample-based planning is one of the finest strategies that scale well to bigger and more complicated issues. The following is how it works:

- Place points at random on the map's free spaces.
- If feasible, connect each point to its nearest neighbors.
- Determine the quickest path via the points to the finish line.

This navigation challenge is at the core of artificial intelligence in robotics. Of fact, the preceding example was only a toy version of the issue. When we add limits and uncertainty, which may involve one or more of the following issues, things get much more difficult.

- The sensors and motors aren't flawless.
- Humans and other elements of the environment continue to obstruct progress.
- The robot does not know where it is and/or does not have a comprehensive map. This is known as the SLAM issue (simultaneous localization and mapping) by roboticists.
- We are concerned about physical restrictions on speed and acceleration since the robot is moving so quickly. Mechanical engineers can help with this.
- There are several robots.

In general, if the robot has a lot of moving components, the task becomes exponentially more difficult. I won't go into too much detail since this is a really abstract issue, but the point is that the planning for each moving portion occurs as if we had added new dimensions to the map. This is due to the robot's requirement for a plan for each coupled joint and motor. The point robot in our example issue navigates in two dimensions: up/down and left/right. A basic humanoid robot must traverse around two dozen dimensions.

Does this imply that AI researchers have learned to think in dimensions other than three? They're not magicians, they're scientists.

Distances and collision avoidance are very difficult to calculate in this strange high-dimensional search space. That's where sophisticated mathematical heuristics come in, and its why robotic motion planning is such a great AI task.

Artificial Intelligence is being used almost everywhere these days. On screens, in pockets, and who knows, maybe one day it'll stroll into a house near you. The headlines tend to condense this vast range into a single topic. Robots produced in laboratories, algorithms winning conventional games, AI and some of the things it can do are becoming a part of our daily lives. Although the majority of these incidents are related to AI, this is not a single discipline, but rather a collection of them.

Artificial intelligence and photonics have enabled the development of robots that use novel techniques for connecting business, medical, and a variety of other applications. There is no denying that the robot era has here. The concept of robots may conjure up images of iconic androids such as C-3PO from "Star Wars" and Rosie from "The Jetsons." It may even instill terror among humans as powerful robots continue to improve and become necessary. The majority of these robots have now taken on risky or dull professions formerly performed by humans. In any event, many people have yet to recognize the pervasiveness of robots since, in many cases, the robots resemble industrial equipment rather than Android.

Robotics exist in every industry, beginning with industrial processing equipment like Google's self-driving vehicle and incorporating photonics technology such as sensors, lasers, and face recognition technology.

According to the International Federation of Robotics (IFR), 2013 saw a growth in the sale of industrial robots in the chemical, automotive, and food processing sectors. One-third of all industrial robots used in automobile manufacture is found in the automotive industry. According to IFR, the worldwide demand for personal and domestic service robots climbed to $1.7 billion between 2012 and 2013.

The traditional character of robots has also resulted in significant advances. For example, when it was revealed that a hotel in Japan would be outfitted with a human-like robot, the notion of squishy humanoid robots from "Future World" or "Westworld" began to take shape.

The "Henn-na Hotel in Nagasaki Prefecture," which translates to "Strange Hotel," was to be outfitted with receptionist robots that resemble humans. These robots were required to welcome guests and engage them in intelligent dialogues. Room service, housekeeping, and porter service were also to be provided by robots.

The Baxter family of robots from Rethink Robotics Inc. in Boston is another less human and more rational robot. Baxter offers an excellent interactive platform that integrates 360-degree sonar sensors with customized software. Baxter continues to operate despite the fact that it has excellent employees that can improve the research and production processes.

Baxter's camera supports computer vision applications with a 30-fps picture capture rate and a high resolution of 640 x 400 pixels.

During the opening of the Australian Centre for Robotic Vision, Sue Keay, the ACRV's chief operating officer, said that robotic vision is the primary technology that would enable robots to alter labor-intensive sectors and overcome stagnant markets. As a result, robots will become a common sight in today's society.

Robots and Artificial Intelligence

'Autonomous technology' and 'artificial intelligence' have grown in popularity in the first two decades of the twenty-first century.

Drones, self-driving vehicles, space exploration, software agents, and deep learning in medical diagnostics are some of the most well-known applications of artificial intelligence. Some of the life areas that have propelled advancement include artificial intelligence in the form of machine learning and the availability of large datasets.

The convergence of these digital technologies has increased their potency. AI deployed in these systems may assist redefine or enhance human situations while reducing the need for human participation and intervention during operation. As a result, smart technology is replacing people in hard, filthy, dull, and hazardous labor.

Smart systems may ease communication with consumers in online contact centers, drive robot hands to precisely pick and operate products, and acquire and sell merchandise in massive numbers in the blink of an eye, all without any direct human participation or external control.

Regardless, it is unfortunate that some of the most effective cognitive tools are essentially opaque. Humans do not program their behaviors in sequential order. Google Brain creates AI, which is apparently superior to humans.

Machine Learning, and Artificial Intelligence
IoT

The Internet of linked things will proliferate in the next decades as these gadgets become more affordable and solar energy cells develop. The Internet Protocol (IP) allows for a maximum of 4,294,967,269 IP addresses in the IPv4 namespace. IPv4 addresses are 32 bits long, totaling 232 bits. The protocol only allows for a limited number of address combinations.

The much newer and better IPv6 protocol, on the other hand, employs 128-bit addresses and, as you would expect, gives orders of magnitude more addresses. In reality, there are around 10 to the 22nd power addresses, which is a staggering quantity. One of the reasons for implementing IPv6 was that the world was running out of IP addresses to utilize for websites. Another reason is that the Internet of Things adds a substantial number of linked devices, all of which need unique IP addresses. With IPv6, the world is prepared to bear the weight of the Internet of Things.

In recent years, consumer Internet of Things penetration has been significant. The so-called "smart home" revolution has seen the emergence of internet-connected smart gadgets such as thermostats, garage openers, toasters, microwaves, TVs, and refrigerators. These devices often have a common interface or dashboard that may be customized using a smartphone.

Why would anybody want to purchase a typical home equipment that is internet-connected? It's a reasonable question and one that marketing teams all across the globe had to consider when these goods were created. The advantages of having an internet connection are evident for certain equipment but less so for others. A smart fridge with a barcode scanner can keep track of the family food supply and notify you when things are ready to expire. The companion smartphone app can then keep track of all food purchases made during the year and provide basic statistics. Technically savvy users may look for a means to export their data for further study. As you would expect, these items are on the pricey side and are marketed to middle and upper-class homes.

Household automation, a broader term, refers to the equipment, technology, and control systems that help in the home economy. At the most basic level, there are garage openers and clap-on lights. Lighting systems, home theater systems, and climate control are located somewhere in the center. At the top end, you get items that are only restricted by the owner's DIY attitude. A skilled person, such as an engineer, may imagine an automatic pet feeder system that only needs food to be replaced once in a while rather than at each meal.

Consumer irrigation systems may also have a "smart" component, such as a dashboard interface with choices for adjusting watering frequency and so on. FarmBot is an autonomous home gardening device that needs very little maintenance. It has the architecture of a CNC milling machine but is supplied with trowels and seed dibblers instead. While the base kit might cost up to $3,500, the business claims that the technology is 100% open-source. This is consistent with the DIY mentality that underpins many Internet of Things devices. Home security system sales have also increased in recent years. Many technology firms are capitalizing on the Internet of Things revolution in the security area, and customers have a variety of brands to select from. Amazon Echo and Alexa, for example, have grown in popularity.

They help with home automation by listening to user instructions and performing some functions. This might be anything from surfing the web to making a shopping list to listening to music.

The user may associate "Alexa skills," which are programmed scripts that the devices execute after each command. These abilities are easily searchable online, and anybody with programming knowledge understands how to publish them.

Home automation is particularly important for the aging population since the requirements of the elderly are many while they live at home. For others, systems may postpone the need for admission to a healthcare institution.

However, with the present technology, these devices can only do so much. Wheelchair stairlifts have been available for many years. Home automation is not a new concept, but it has acquired increased popularity with the Internet of Things technology. There are several advantages to applying Internet of Things ideas to home automation for the elderly. One of the most crucial elements that many senior homeowners want is an alarm system that can dial 911 if they become disabled.

Non-emergency notifications, such as reminders to take medications and schedule doctor's visits, are also beneficial. A real application of the Internet of Things methodology would involve a smart gadget worn on the wrist or chest that delivers information about heart rate and blood pressure to the patient's doctor. Recent advancements in smart fabric technology enable this capability to be built directly into the patient's clothing. These technologies will be able to combine with robots in the future to provide extra support.

Domestic robots will cook meals, clean up after the sick, and help with tasks.

The industrial sector is home to yet another innovative family of Internet of Things applications. Weather conditions, equipment status, and logistics may all be sent through smart sensors. RFID technology can monitor stock-keeping units (SKUs) as they travel from warehouse to warehouse. The "industrial internet" brings together networked equipment, big data analytics, and real-time updates. These always-on measures are very inexpensive for huge corporations like General Electric to install while providing a lot of information. Operators may immediately identify areas where the industrial or manufacturing process causes inefficiency.

When a bottleneck is found, the required modifications to fix it are prioritized. By optimizing the whole process, increasing the number of linked devices reduces sunk costs in the form of productivity losses. When you have access to all of the world's data, you have alternatives. Despite the fact that General Electric is an industrial internet giant, the notion has achieved modest worldwide acceptance.

The use of Internet of Things devices in the establishment of "smart grids" for common utilities has also been advocated. The goal is to employ monitoring devices to evaluate the amount of power demand so that the grid may direct resources to places in most need while also increasing efficiency. This allows the utility supplier and the customer to communicate in both directions. Smart grids will eventually result in cheaper power bills for consumers and widespread availability for everybody. The replacement of outdated equipment with new is a hidden advantage of upgrading power networks into smart grids. It is no secret that the infrastructure of the United States is deteriorating. Installing new networked devices provides policymakers with a reason to finally get rid of unwanted components. A modern grid is a more secure and dependable grid.

Existing machine learning algorithms will only get smarter as the Internet of Things technologies produces vast volumes of data. If a corporation is already harvesting data from sensors and other connected devices, you can bet that it is being stored in a data lake or data warehouse solution. High bandwidth data ingestion engines are required for real-time analytics to digest information as it is transmitted to servers. Big data is expected to expand in tandem with the deployment of these networked devices. The internet as it now exists creates vast amounts of data. Every minute, social media applications like Snapchat and Instagram post hundreds of user-generated photographs and videos. Facebook, LinkedIn, Quora, and others produce data for each user via user postings, as well as in-house and third-party analytics. Almost every high-traffic website employs third-party monitoring and data harvesting plugins. These track mouse movements, keystrokes, and clicks on advertising banners. Essentially, every activity taken by a human agent on a signed-in account may create data for a variety of firms.

When you include the Internet of Things, which generates multiple sorts of data formats based on wireless technologies, the global data glut skyrockets. The World Wide Web, for example, employs a variety of data formats that are widely known to data scientists. JSON, CSV (comma-separated values), and XML are examples of these. Many devices linked through web protocols such as HTTP interact with this form of columnar data. In 2020, the number of connected devices is estimated to reach 31 billion. That is over 30 times the current number of individuals online. In 2017, the quantity of data generated by these connected citizens was estimated to be approximately 2.5 quintillion bytes per day. We may anticipate new approaches and algorithms to be introduced to the already broad repertory of limited artificial intelligence as the area of machine learning expands. Because linked devices may be almost anything, it is impossible to predict how they will be used. We do, however, have a basic idea of where things are headed. Sensing, communication, and relaying are the three most fundamental concepts of the Internet of Things technology. As a result, the Internet of Things will be utilized to build large-scale communications networks comprised of tiny objects.

Only time will tell whether the security posture of the Internet of Things can be strengthened to the point where regulators are more inclined to accept them.

Continued research into the safety of vehicle networks will need to improve before governments can approve roadside vehicular sensors. The same is true for smart grids. As you read this, smart city experiments are taking place all around the world. A quick Google search might put you in the correct direction for such a city near you. In any event, in the future decades, you can expect to hear more about Internet of Things security, deployment, vehicular networks, and legislation. Any new technology is generally reluctant to catch on, but when it does, it has the potential to transform society.

The confluence of AI and AI progress with IoT is a critical part of artificial intelligence that business executives must be aware of. Indeed, IoT is one of the elements of our modern era that has enabled the AI revolution to occur. What is the Internet of Things? Some may be acquainted with the Internet of Things (IoT), while others may not. IoT stands for Internet of Things, and it refers to the internet connection that many contemporary gadgets have.

The electronics in concern go beyond mobile phones, laptop computers, portable music players, and TVs. We are approaching the point when every electrical gadget in a home will almost certainly have an internet connection in the near future. This implies a desire not just to enhance the functioning of these items, but also to control them with virtual assistants or to generate revenue possibilities for AI providers.

One day, virtual assistant software will be able to make you a hot cup of coffee when you arrive home, turn on the fireplace so your living room is toasty (just the way you like it), possibly start the shower for you (even adjusting the shower head to your desired massage level), and adjust your bed to the proper angle to accommodate your back problems. To someone who is unfamiliar with computer science and AI, these kinds of capabilities seem to be simply a matter of updating Alexa and other virtual assistants to be able to perform these sorts of things, but there is much more to this type of setup than that.

Not only must the virtual assistant be capable of communicating with the device (ostensibly via wireless internet), but the device must also be capable of communicating back in a language that the virtual assistant understands, the device must be linked to an AI or cloud that can monitor data points, and a human operator must be able to use the device as well, possibly even overriding the commands that the device receives from the AI virtual manager. Do you see the issue here?

Because of the fast-evolving IoT environment, many regularly used gadgets in the home or workplace are likely to be linked to the internet in order to be controlled by AI, such as virtual assistants. However, this implies that these devices will be storing data in ways they may not have before, and this data storage may involve data monitoring on the cloud. Again, this is a security problem since not only the AI, but also operators at the AI firm (who may store and monitor the data on their servers), and hackers may be able to access data about your devices simply because they have all been connected to AI.

Some may see the potential for difficulties right away. The purpose of this conversation was not to emphasize the difficulties but to explain why business leaders should be thinking about IoT, although it is also vital for business leaders to consider the challenges. If you work in a company that utilizes IoT to perform business operations, you should be aware of how you might be held accountable for data that your AI accesses and manipulates in order to control other devices. This is a point that the reader will be reminded of many times. AI does provide a degree of data danger, and organizations must consider how to manage that risk.

Of course, the worst-case scenario is that people who have all of their domestic equipment connected to AI may encounter a Gremlins-like situation. You know what we mean: some evil entity (perhaps the AI itself) turns all of your home appliances against you because they have a grudge against you or are just driven by a desire to do something awful. Isn't that what the movie Gremlins was all about? The Gremlins reflected the worst aspects of human nature in the shape of a monstrous beast that burst out laughing as it plowed people over with a snow plow.

Fear underpins part of the AI debate, although it may be less significant in the hard scientific arena of artificial intelligence. Indeed, the scientific approach to AI argues that AI will be basically benevolent and that the majority of concern around AI stems from a lack of knowledge of artificial intelligence. Of fact, this final argument regarding AI does not stand up under investigation, since some of the most vocal opponents of AI are also experts in the field. Stephen Hawking and Elon Musk are not ordinary folks. These are scientists and engineers who comprehend what AI is capable of and why there may be some reason to be concerned.

The preceding book in this series discusses the concern around AI (and whether these worries were justified). The goal of this talk at this point is to give the reader a sense of what IoT entails in terms of artificial intelligence. It implies that for a virtual assistant AI to operate your gadgets and appliances, they must be connected to the internet. Connecting these gadgets to the internet and storing data on a cloud or a corporate server poses yet another security concern for AI that business executives should keep in the back of their minds.

Of course, depending on how you want to utilize AI, IoT may be of more or lesser importance to you. Perhaps you are developing a dating website, with consumers accessing your firm's site through an app on their phones or browser. In this scenario, your privacy concerns are typical of those associated with AI-powered applications. It is critical that you grasp them, but they are not the overwhelming difficulties that some other company executives and computer scientists face.

However, whether you work in heavy industry or another business that uses artificial intelligence-enabled equipment, IoT is something you should consider, even though it may not seem clear at first. For example, if you want to automate your operations by having AI run your heavy gear, you are entering the IoT realm. This is also true for companies that utilize drones to monitor production sites, plants, equipment, people, and so on. Artificial intelligence is very certainly speaking with these gadgets through the internet (even if it is not in human language), and this data is being kept someplace and might possibly be accessed by someone you do not want to see it.

IoT's Growing Importance

One of the most visible manifestations of AI culture is the growing importance of the Internet of Things or IoT, and we don't only mean smartphones, smart speakers, smart automobiles, and other apparent instances of an everyday technology that have now been linked to the internet. Tech businesses are experimenting with new methods to make culture more internet- and information-driven. Companies have created smartwatches with internet connections and several smartphone functions, as well as glasses that project information onto lenses. Another area in which IoT is growing is headpieces and possibly implanted devices. Even Facebook has suggested creating implanted gadgets that would enable users to receive messages or notifications instantaneously.

This implies that leaders and teams will need to keep up not just with AI developments when they are announced, but also with the development of these improvements. In other words, as soon as a concept for a certain form of technology is proposed, organizations must consider how they may use that idea or how it might affect them. Because the trend of more gadgets connecting to the internet is not going away anytime soon, companies have both obstacles and opportunities when it comes to capturing markets for themselves.

Business adaption will be determined by how successful executives are able to develop a culture conducive to artificial intelligence in their operations.

Intelligent coordination and control are required for all IoT devices. The recent decade witnessed enormous advances in AI systems that can collaborate with IoT regardless of disparities.

AI looks to be the most intriguing issue right now. There are a lot of discussions, and even some misunderstandings and confusion, concerning what AI is and is not. AI is having an impact on both existing and future businesses throughout the globe. It is not fleeing and is expected to become more significant as it expands.

The Internet of Things (IoT) refers to an ecosystem of discrete computer devices that employ sensors and are linked through Internet infrastructure. The concept has been brewing in the industry for some time, but the democratization of computer technology via the cost and availability of tiny computing devices propelled it to the forefront.

Artificial intelligence is producing a wave in the Internet of Things (IoT) due to increased investment, the development of new technologies, and the rising tide of business installations.

Signals

1. AI venture capital financing is rapidly increasing.

2. AI-focused IoT start-ups are being acquired in large numbers.

3. Big enterprises across sectors are already using AI and IoT to provide new solutions and perform more effectively.

The AI Key to Unlocking IoT Potential

Artificial intelligence plays a significant role in IoT applications and deployments. In the past two years, both acquisitions and investments in firms that merge AI and IoT have surged. Key IoT platform software suppliers now offer integrated AI capabilities such as machine learning analytics.

The importance of AI in this context stems from its ability to quickly extract insights from data. Machine learning, an AI technique, allows intelligent sensors and equipment to automatically detect patterns and discover abnormalities in data such as humidity, temperature, vibration, and sound.

When compared to typical business intelligence devices that monitor numeric thresholds, machine learning algorithms may provide operational predictions up to 20 times faster and with more accuracy.

Other AI technologies, such as voice recognition and computer vision, may help with data analysis. AI applications for IoT enable businesses to avoid unexpected downtime, develop new products, boost productivity, and improve risk management.

AI and IoT Collaboration

AI and IoT have unique histories but are in the same evolutionary stage.

They all began with the intention of improving outdated systems. This refers to automating and upgrading available infrastructure and procedures for greater production and efficiency in the context of the Internet of Things.

When it comes to Artificial Intelligence, the first applications put a strong focus on human-centered operations. Nowadays, the trend is toward an integrated IoT native and AI-native approach that is built from the bottom up to support transformational digital approaches.

In most situations, new IoT solutions have built-in functionalities.

Some of the significance and advancements brought forth by AI include:

AI and IoT enable automation, which disrupts the labor market by creating a need for a new and distinct set of skills across a wide range of sectors. Accommodation, manufacturing, transportation, and food services are some of the sectors in the United States that have been revolutionized by shifting responsibilities.

AI and IoT enable the creation of new value propositions.

AI's Role in the Internet of Things

Artificial intelligence has been more important in the last year if you want to construct and expand the number of sensor online devices. It will be much more critical when you wish to derive meaning from data transmitted from the same devices to aid the IoT revolution.

The Quantified Self and the Internet of Things Revolution

The concept of the "quantified self" helps us grasp the beginning of the convergence of IoT and AI. In other terms, quantified self refers to personal information gained via technology-assisted self-tracking. Do we have a nice life? How can you make it better?

Where should we spend our time?

You acquire data in a variety of aspects of your life. You may examine inputs like the quality of the air around us, as well as various stages of our emotions. We seem concerned about our mental and physical health at times.

However, data is the most valuable resource for us since it may lead to action. This implies that you must gather and evaluate data as soon as possible in order to maintain a constant flow of information. This is one of the primary processes that lead to the Internet of Things revolution.

IoT necessitates the use of artificial intelligence.

According to 2020 forecasts, there will be many linked devices per person; data processed will be in gigabytes per second, not including IoT. At some time, the Internet of Things will be the greatest source of data in the world. And the Internet of Things revolution may enable gadgets to highlight possibilities.

You now understand how information technologies aid in the transition from legacy systems to advanced intelligent applications and services. It is critical to develop real-time data collection in order to choose the previously recognized pattern. However, finding a way to deal with this, as well as the data and information created by these devices, is a huge challenge.

AI in the IoT Revolution

IoT is presently producing a massive haystack of data. Many companies are having difficulty making sense of massive volumes of data. Each big organization collects and maintains a vast amount of human-oriented data about its consumers, including their purchases, preferences, and other personal information.

Finally, the Internet of Things refers to data transfer between devices. Artificial intelligence is required to discover these needles in a haystack. Artificial intelligence may become a significant component of any IoT system in the coming years.

Artificial Intelligence Ethics

Because of the many advantages it provides, artificial intelligence has become a modern-day phenomenon. Artificial intelligence (AI) has both advantages and disadvantages in the commercial environment. AI algorithms are being used by businesses to improve their company performance, profitability, and productivity. The use of solutions powered by Machine Learning and Artificial Intelligence applications has grown quite prevalent. However, this does not imply that Artificial Intelligence is without challenges for organizations.

Artificial intelligence poses various concerns, including:

Data Accessibility

During the implementation phase of AI, data is often of poor quality and inconsistent, making it difficult to get value from AI.

Skills Scarcity

Businesses attempting to use AI may face a skills shortage; there may be a dearth of competent technical people. This might result in additional expenditures for training staff to ensure the effective functioning of AI.

Artificial intelligence implementation is expensive.

To keep AI robots working efficiently, software packages must be updated on a regular basis. When there is a personnel shortage, firms are obliged to outsource, which is expensive. The extra expenditures required in data training models may be highly expensive, particularly for small organizations.

Other artificial intelligence limitations include:

Depending on the Artificial Intelligence systems being deployed, there may be delays in the implementation process.

Misunderstanding Artificial Intelligence programs leads to integration difficulties.

When AI applications interact with other programs, they may not perform properly.

These hazards demanded the creation and subsequent application of artificial intelligence company safety, legislation, universal data protection regulation, and ethics. Because of the huge risk potential linked with AI ethics, a framework charged with its management has been established.

What are some of the fundamental principles that guide governments, companies, and developers in the ethical deployment of AI-powered systems?

Creating net advantages

Artificial Intelligence systems need to function by providing advantages to consumers that outweigh the hazards.

There is no damage done.

Artificial intelligence must be created in such a manner that humans are neither misled nor hurt and bad effects are minimized.

Compliance with the law and regulations

Artificial intelligence systems must comply with all government commitments, rules, and laws.

Privacy protection for users

Artificial intelligence systems are obligated to ensure that data is kept secret and secure. When deploying AI systems, harmful data breaches must be avoided.

Fairness

Individuals, companies, and communities that use Artificial Intelligence technology must not face unjust discrimination. These systems should be constructed in such a way that they do not generate injustice due to training biases.

Transparency and explain ability

Users must be fully informed about how the AI algorithms utilized influence them. Users must have a thorough comprehension of the data or information that these algorithms rely on to make conclusions.

Contestability

Because algorithms directly influence consumers, a competent procedure that may dispute their output or use must be in place.

Accountability

Organizations and individuals are responsible for the creation and deployment of Artificial Intelligence algorithms must be held accountable and identified for the effect of the algorithms. This is true regardless of whether the effects are planned or inadvertent.

How does the General Data Protection Regulation (GDPR) protect users in the age of artificial intelligence?

1) GDPR in terms of privacy protection

The General Data Protection Regulation creates a stumbling block in the application of AI. At the same time, it is a significant aspect when it comes to consumer privacy. As a consequence of data breaches, trust in data privacy has been weakened. The good news about this danger in Artificial Intelligence is that organizations may regain lost confidence simply by adhering to GDPR. This implies that businesses adopt a basic approach to Artificial Intelligence privacy.

GDPR states that keeping data for longer than required is not permissible. This raises the issue of whether or not Artificial Intelligence is being muted. This may be perplexing since AI mainly depends on prior data to interpret information that allows the system to make judgments.

2) GDPR implementation in automated profiling and decision making

GDPR has special regulations that address judgments based on artificial intelligence, specifically automated profiling and decision-making. Set requirements must be properly followed to guarantee that users are not influenced.

3) GDRP in data collection

As far as GDPR is concerned, the first step is to ensure that the organization properly knows the data that is gathered and how the data is handled. It is critical to document the data type acquired, as well as the source and routes via which it was collected.

4) The use of GDRP in risk assessment

A Data Protection Impact Assessment (DPIA) must be completed before using automated decision-making. DPIA enables the company to assess the risks associated with automated decision-making. DPIA strives to examine risks to data subjects at each stage of data processing.

5) GDRP and third-party management

It is critical to understand the privacy and security protections used by your provider. Check with your vendor to see whether he has all of the needed industry qualifications; this is critical in the verification of vendor evaluations.

Finally, the Artificial Intelligence and General Data Protection Regulation highlights that the vast data employed in AI is directly opposed to the intended limiting of data preservation and gathering. It is obvious that, in terms of AI user safety, according to established rules aids in the protection of users' privacy.

 Ensure that your providers follow these requirements to the letter prior to AI adoption. This may seem to be a difficult process, but the good news is that people feel safer and more secure in dealing with your organization when they know they are protected.

Privacy Protection and Artificial Intelligence

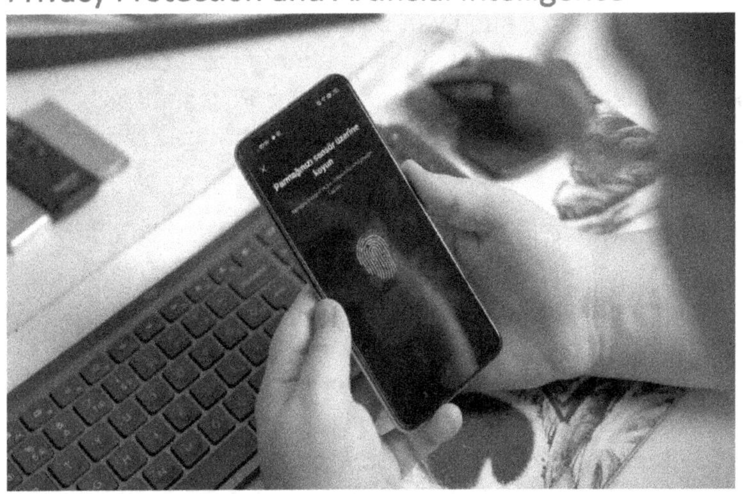

Security is a major worry for the traditional Internet, and it is a hotly debated one for the Internet of Things.

Many individuals are worried that the business is advancing too quickly and without enough discussion of the security risks inherent in these devices and their networks. In addition to the normal security problems encountered on the Internet, the Internet of Things has new difficulties – security controls in the industry, Internet of Things business processes, hybrid systems, and end nodes.

The major worry with implementing Internet of Things technology is most likely security. Cyber-attacks against industrial components are predicted to rise as the size of IoT usage grows. And these dangers are more likely to become actual rather than virtual.

Many security flaws exist in today's Internet of Things systems, including a lack of encrypted communication between devices, weak authentication (many devices are allowed to run in production environments with default credentials), a lack of verification or encryption of software updates, and even SQL injection. Bad actors may leverage these vulnerabilities to simply steal user passwords, intercept data and acquire Personally Identifiable Information, or even implant malware into upgraded firmware.

Much internet-connected equipment, including kitchen appliances, thermostats, cameras, and TVs, is already spying on individuals in their own homes. Many contemporary automotive components, including dashboard displays, the horn, heating/cooling, hood and trunk releases, the engine, door locks, and even brakes, are vulnerable to manipulation if a bad actor gains access to the vehicle's onboard systems. Wireless remote assaults are possible on automobiles that have a wireless connection. Attacks against other internet-connected devices, such as insulin pumps, implanted cardioverter defibrillators, and pacemakers, have also been shown. Because some of these devices have significant space and computing power limits, they may be unable to utilize typical security measures such as strong encryption for communication or even firewalls.

Concerns about privacy in the Internet of Things are divided into two categories: acceptable and illegitimate applications. In lawful applications, governments and major enterprises may build up vast IoT services that, by definition, capture tremendous quantities of data. This data may be exploited in a variety of ways by a private organization, with little or no redress for the individuals whose lives and actions are caught up in the data collection. Massive data gathering from the Internet of Things networks provides governments with the data they need to deliver services and infrastructure, conserve resources and cut emissions, and so on. Simultaneously, these systems will gather massive quantities of data about people, such as their locations, activities, buying habits, travel, and so on. This, according to some, is the establishment of a genuine surveillance state. It is impossible to reject this claim without a legal framework in place to prohibit governments from just scooping up infinite quantities of data to deal with as they like.

Illegal applications of the large Internet of Things networks range from DDOS (distributed denial of service) assaults to malware attacks on one or more of the network's IoT devices.

Worryingly, security flaws in even one device on an Internet of Things network can, by virtue of the fact that it is capable of full communication with all devices nearby because it has access to the encryption requirements to present itself as a legitimate device on the network, mean that an infected device may not only provide its illegitimate host with the data it provides, but also metadata of other devices in the network, and possibly even access to the e-commerce platform.

In 2016, a DDOS assault fueled by an Internet of Things device infected with malware infected over 300,000 devices and knocked down a DNS provider as well as numerous large websites. This Mirai Botnet was able to identify attack devices, which were largely IP cameras, DVRs, printers, and routers.

While there are various attempts underway to improve security in the Internet of Things sector, many feel that government regulation and international collaboration are the only ways to secure public safety.

The Security of Using Recommender Systems

Recommender systems may be very accurate forecasters of people's preferences. Their dependence on implicit and explicit user input assists in identifying distinct user preferences but does so at the expense of revealing important information about a person's political beliefs, health condition, sexual orientation, and other private information. In some circumstances, the information gathered and processed is innocuous, such as a user's favorite Internet browser, while in others, the information may be very sensitive, raising issues about personal privacy.

Users looking for sensitive material such as personal well-being, health, and relationship counseling may not feel at ease browsing systems that repurpose their activity to generate suggestions. These choices may eventually be communicated to friends, coworkers, classmates, and family via material and advertisements presented on their screens.

A lady in the American Midwest sued Netflix in 2009 when her sexual preferences were revealed online. The Netflix subscriber sued the business under the alias "Doe" for including her personal information in the 2007 Netflix Prize dataset. The case was launched after scholarly research at the University of Texas revealed privacy issues in the dataset utilized by Netflix for the competition.

Despite Netflix's efforts to erase personal identifiers such as names from the data, the identities were disclosed by comparing the competition's information with film ratings from the publicly accessible Internet Movie Database. With an 84% success rate, the researchers discovered that an anonymous user's rating of six obscure movies might be used to identify an individual Netflix subscriber.

Furthermore, when the date of a movie review was available, the accuracy rate increased to 99%.

In Doe vs. Netflix, the latter was found to have violated US fair trade regulations as well as the Video Privacy Protection Act. The continuing litigation also forced Netflix to cancel the second Netflix Prize competition, which was scheduled for 2010.

Although open data contests and recommender systems have grown in popularity, data privacy remains a delicate topic. In April 2018, Facebook Founder Mark Zuckerberg testified before Congress on his company's data-sharing policy. His attendance on Capitol Hill was part of a hearing investigating Facebook's alleged sharing of voter preferences with a data analytics business that aided the Donald Trump election campaign.

While the examples of Facebook and Netflix both emphasize issues about user data management rather than the usage of particular algorithms (such as those discussed in this book), the present geopolitical atmosphere has implications for the use of recommender systems. The privacy of user data is under examination since it is used to fuel tailored recommender systems. The availability of actual data for open contests is also critical for the industry's growth and the evolution of algorithm-based models, as the inaugural Netflix Prize intended.

However, new restrictions are poised to have a significant influence on firms that gather and keep user data. This covers GDPR, Europe's new internet data privacy regulation. The new legislation increases openness for users in terms of how their data is handled and the use of cookies on online apps, as well as a clearer "right to be forgotten" when users no longer want their data to be stored (if there are no legal reasons for doing so).

GDPR also requires users stored personal data to be encrypted, as well as the right of users to approve or refuse the use of their personal information for the implementation of online recommendations.

Aside from data availability and transparency considerations, there are additional special concerns concerning the usage of recommender systems.

Governments are obviously worried about the rising danger of internet content manipulation, based on recent legislative reforms in Europe, congressional hearings in the United States, and comments from Donald Trump. This includes biased information distribution, state-sponsored groups attempting to influence public mood via paid advertising, and the dissemination of false news on internet platforms.

All three issues are directly related to content-feeding algorithms and the platforms that provide these content display systems. The algorithms that feed material to Facebook users, for example, have no method of distinguishing between false and legitimate news articles, nor do they have the capacity to stay bipartisan in the event of a political election. While it is possible to eliminate recognized sources of incorrect information, there is nothing that can be done to prevent the biases that unavoidably develop from user-collected data, short of avoiding these systems entirely.

Avoidance may be the only choice for certain businesses, such as Napster. Despite demands for the file-sharing site to utilize its access to personal information (of up to 70 million members) to promote music and help in the discovery of lesser-known musicians, the company's management and legal experts rejected the notion. The addition of collaborative filtering, as advocated by music aficionados working as computer engineers at Napster, would have bolstered record companies' assertions that the network was leading users to unlicensed material. Napster, like telecommunications firms that refuse to accept responsibility for illicit acts carried out on their infrastructure, sought to disassociate itself from any type of user misbehavior on their platform.

Napster contended that it was just a platform and hence could not be held liable for the acts of its users. While this ruling did not prevent litigation or the ultimate death of Napster's original service, it does illustrate the legal risks associated with installing recommender systems, particularly collaborative filtering.

Whether motivated by fear of legal repercussions or more philanthropic intentions, all businesses that use customized recommender systems must establish and adhere to a basic code of ethics and compliance. This includes adhering to the rules and regulations of the nations and areas in which they operate and where data is held. Personal data obtained in Mainland China, for example, cannot be transported or retained beyond the Mainland under China's new Cybersecurity Law.

In light of this, the US National Academies are proposing a data science oath, which includes pledges such as "I will respect the privacy of my data subjects" and "I will remember that my data are not just data numbers without meaning or context, but represent real people and situations and that my work may have unintended societal consequences." Other principles called for by the data science ethics community include consent consideration, bias awareness, and data protection against deanonymization.

A realistic first step for firms seeking to reduce legal risk and other public ramifications is to examine what material is submitted to the recommendation engine in the first place. While the ability to influence the output of model-based predictions is restricted, actions may be made to limit the scope of data variables selected for filtering. This may include omitting sensitive criteria such as "marital status" and "race" when predicting credit card application appropriateness or the display of internet adverts.

Furthermore, it is critical to promote corporate openness and ensure that relevant departments such as upper management and legal teams are aware of the factors used to create suggestions as well as the content of what is given to users as output. This is particularly relevant considering the increased scrutiny of what internet platforms propose to consumers.

One of these worried voices is Zeynep Tufekci, an associate professor at the University of North Carolina's School of Information and Library Science, who has exposed YouTube's inclination to steer visitors toward extreme material through its autoplay recommendation system. Tufekci recounted how watching Donald Trump rallies on YouTube lead her to Holocaust denials, rants from white supremacists, and other difficult and disturbing information in a story published in the New York Times in early 2018. Similarly, watching Hillary Clinton and Bernie Sanders videos on a newly created YouTube account led Tufekci to videos that were conspiratorial in nature, such as the secret presence of government agencies and the US government's alleged involvement in the September 11 attacks. In both situations, YouTube suggested material that was increasingly more extreme throughout the duration of Tufekci's user experience, as well as content that was far less mainstream in Tufekci's perspective than in her initial search.

Former Google engineer Guillaume Chaslot has also questioned the parent company's ethics. Chaslot worked on a team at Google that created recommendation algorithms for YouTube. Chaslot cites a tendency toward anti-media material as well as a recommender system that promotes animosity of rival media sources. During the 2016 U.S. election, Chaslot discovered that politicians who were most hostile towards the media were suggested four times more often by YouTube than their opponents.

Chaslot has also pioneered the establishment of algotransparency.org, which provides research tools to educate the public about what drives recommender algorithms like those employed by YouTube. Political elections, mass murders, science, and even the issue of whether the planet is flat are all tracked content subjects. Needless to say, the discussion over the ethical implications of recommender technology will continue to rage in the next years and should be a major priority for data scientists and businesses.

Another key concern for the business is to maintain end-user confidence. User trust may be maintained in nations and places where there is an established culture surrounding data privacy by providing consumers with the option to opt out of utilizing their personal information for predictive screening. Transparency and disclaimers about how and why the site make suggestions to its visitors may also help to build trust.

The labeling of suggested information is one aspect of transparency practice. Researchers in Germany discovered that the labeling style of suggested goods greatly influenced consumers' responses in the 2013 study article Sponsored vs. Organic Recommendations and the Impact of Labeling. According to the research, the click-through rate for suggested material labeled "Sponsored" was 5.93%, while it was 8.86% when the same content was branded "Organic." The clickthrough rate for content without a label was 9.87%.

According to this study, labeling suggested material is not always in the best interests of internet platforms or marketers.

The precise click-through and response rate of labeled item suggestions, however, may vary among platforms and use cases. Some platforms take advantage of transparency. This includes Spotify, whose users are lured in part by the awareness that other users' interests aid in music discovery.

Finally, the sensitivity of recommender systems may vary from innocuous and insignificant to legally risky and detrimental to an organization's long-term performance. Understanding where your recommender engine falls on the spectrum of possible legal repercussions and their influence on user confidence is critical. The answer will be highly influenced by the data variables you choose to collect and process, how you store and utilize that information, the amount of operational transparency you give internally, and what you decide to expose to your end users externally.

Is Artificial Intelligence Risky?

To gain a sense of how significant Artificial Intelligence is in our everyday lives, consider what aspects of our contemporary lifestyle have not been affected by it. The "intelligent machines" meant to augment human capacities and improve efficiency are influencing every aspect of human existence. Artificial intelligence is the key premise of the Fourth Industrial Revolution, and it has the capacity to challenge our understanding of what it means to be "human."

Here are a few examples of why Artificial Intelligence is vital for your organization right now:

· Automation of data-driven repeated learning and discovery.

Unlike hardware-driven robotic automation, which tends to automate manual operations, AI consistently and reliably executes high-frequency, high-volume computer-based tasks. However, for AI automation, human inquiry is still required to set up the system and ask important questions.

· Adding intelligence to existing goods. AI would be utilized to augment the capabilities of goods that we currently use, similar to how Siri was introduced to the next generation of iPhones. AI cannot be sold as a self-contained application. Home and workplace technologies, such as investment analysis and network security, may be considerably enhanced by merging vast amounts of data with automation, smart equipment, robotics, and conversational platforms.

· AI will be able to adapt to a changing reality thanks to progressive learning algorithms. Machine learning enables the computer to learn, make notes, and improve upon its mistakes. AI discovers structure and patterns in data to assist the algorithm in learning, allowing the system to operate as a classifier or predictor. The algorithm can educate itself on what online things to promote next, just as it has taught itself how to play chess. The beauty of this model is that it adapts to new data sets. If the initial answer is considered erroneous, an AI approach known as Backpropagation enables the model to modify based on the fresh data and training.

· AI is analyzing deeper and bigger data sets via the use of neural networks with several hidden layers. Consider this: a fraud detection system with several hidden levels could only be imagined a few years ago. A completely new world awaits us with the arrival of big data and hitherto unimagined computing capacities. Data is like gas to computers; the more data you can give them, the quicker and more precise the outcomes. Deep learning models thrive on an abundance of data since they learn directly from it.

· The deep neural networks of AI have reached unbelievable precision. For example, since Alexa and Google Search are based on deep learning, the more we use them, the more accurate they become. Deep neural networks are also advancing our medical area. Image classification and object recognition can now detect cancer on MRIs with the same accuracy as a highly trained doctor.

· AI assists in extracting the most value from data. Data is becoming its own currency, and when algorithms learn on their own, it may quickly become intellectual property. The raw data is analogous to a gold mine: the more and deeper you dig, the more gold, or relevant information, you may extract. Simply adding AI to data may help you get the correct answers quicker, giving you a competitive edge. Even if everyone is using the same methodology, the best data will always triumph.

• The rapid application of AI technology enables new innovations to be launched at an extraordinarily quick speed, making it impossible to stay up. It is becoming more necessary for more people to fully comprehend the ramifications of AI on our planet.

• The significance of artificial intelligence on our civilization cannot be overstated. As we extend the scope and use of AI in the world around us, it will undoubtedly enhance, alter, or create things we cannot yet envision.

• Technology behemoths such as "Google" and "Amazon" are actively investing in AI research and development, demonstrating the significance of AI for companies in general and, by extension, the whole economy.

• AI will have legal ramifications all throughout the world, with governments needing to examine and amend their laws and regulations in light of AI policy. The usage of AI in healthcare and transportation will need government supervision of the protected data utilized by AI.

• Strong cooperation between the private and public sectors worldwide, not just huge tech corporations, is required to properly use AI to better serve mankind. Our travel and hotel sectors are already undergoing this transformation.

A debate about humanized artificial intelligence inevitably leads to the prediction issue of whether artificial intelligence will resemble human intellect in the future or merely "humanness." Some of the concerns regarding artificial intelligence may arise from philosophical assumptions about the nature of humans or existence in general. If the cosmos is regarded as an inherently good creation (or just a thing that exists), and people, like other forms of life, are conceived as being good, then there is no reason to conclude that artificial intelligence presents an intrinsic risk to humanity.

However, if the world is viewed to be ambiguous, a creation that is neither good nor terrible and in which good and bad things sometimes interact to the disadvantage of one or the other, then artificial intelligence becomes potentially deadly. If we actually live in a "dog eat dog" society, the perils of developing something smarter than ourselves and resistant to many of our flaws are evident. If humans abuse the species under their supervision as individuals at the top of the food chain, how can we expect robots not to mistreat us?

These kinds of concerns provide a philosophical slant to the artificial intelligence discussion that is frequently overlooked.

Although the problem with artificial intelligence seems to be whether or not we as humans can trust computers enough to provide them with capacities higher than our own, the actual issue is one of human nature itself. The implicit premise driving AI worries is that artificial intelligence will someday become human-like and that this prospect is terrifying.

It is necessary to highlight fictional depictions of artificial intelligence.

Artificially intelligent robots (and the artificially intelligent systems that guide them) are portrayed in films such as The Terminator as thinking in the same manner that humans do. In other words, human-type thinking holds that humans are harmful to the ecosystem or the cosmos as a whole and should be eradicated. This reasoning states, "This thing is bad; we should get rid of it." However, it is impossible to predict how conscious computers (thinking machines powered by artificial intelligence) might view humans.

A person may eliminate all weeds from a garden because the weeds are harmful to flowers or crops, or a human may kill foxes and wolves because of the threat these creatures provide to farm animals and cattle. This does not necessarily imply that an artificially intelligent computer would act similarly. If a sugar cane plantation is managed by an artificially intelligent computer with the purpose of increasing productivity, the AI software may reach the same conclusion that a person would: this specific item is hazardous to the plantation and should be eliminated. But suppose the program concludes that the sugar plantation itself is superfluous: that sweet goods are unnecessary and that we should stop cultivating them.

Or maybe the machine will learn where to grow things that we as humans do not have.

Humans have wiped off plant and animal species in order to develop farmland or settlements. humans know that there are issues with the way humans interact with our surroundings, and many AI theorists believe that artificial intelligence will reach the same conclusion. Perhaps they would, but they may have recommendations or answers that humans have not considered. Just like humans developed new food sources for them to consume over tens of thousands of years, artificial intelligence agents may develop new food sources or new methods of cultivating food that alleviate many of the difficulties that humans face today.

The robots that dominate the Earth in the film The Matrix ultimately conclude that humans are a great source of energy, and the machines maintain humans in a collective hallucination in order to soothe and sedate them. However, this image of robots suggests that computers would have the same motives as humans. Humans' connection with other species on the earth, for example, is defined by a decrease in habitats and the number of competing species with the explicit goal of furthering human interest. A film like The Matrix predicts that robots would interact with humans and other creatures in this self-serving manner.

In reality, this perception of artificial intelligence acting in this somewhat malevolent human manner – hunting humans to extinction or turning us into fodder – assumes that thinking machines are motivated by the same essential motivations that drive apex species in the animal kingdom. As much as we as humans may believe in our superiority and holiness as a species, we fundamentally act in an animalistic manner.

We've mastered it to the point that we've surpassed the other creatures in our surroundings.

A human family, for example, moves into a wooded region where a bear lives. After many events in which the bear enters the human house, drawn by the scent of food or anything else, the family decides to take action against the bear.

Similarly, if deer populations rise in a rural region for a variety of human-related causes, the state or county Department of natural resources chooses to begin culling deer numbers due to concerns about deer-related accidents, deer incursion into human habitats, and so on. What underpins all of these relationships is the belief that human interests trump the interests of other species. Instead of relocating to avoid the bear, the family decides that the simplest thing to do is to eliminate the bear. Our intentions as humans are typically not led by a desire for balance with our surroundings but by a desire to promote our interests in the environment to the greatest degree possible.

Though we may create artificial intelligence with the purpose of making it human-like or humanized, we expect that fully conscious artificial intelligence - AI that exceeds its programming and acts independently of humans - would behave similarly to how we do. Perhaps it won't. Perhaps artificial intelligence will be able to attain equilibrium with the global environment in ways that humans cannot.

The goal here is not to argue that artificial intelligence is superior to humans, but rather to raise the philosophical issue of what the motives of artificially intelligent life might be.

When we presume that artificial intelligence will have the same self-centered goals as humans, we are assuming that humans are the ideal species on Earth and that any rival will naturally resemble us in some manner. This is not always the case.

Although artificial intelligence might (and most likely will) achieve human-like cognitive capacities, this does not imply that they would think like humans and reach the same conclusions. When we suggest that artificially intelligent robots might possibly kill the human race, we are essentially arguing that if we possessed the powers that machines would have, we would annihilate humans.

Existentially, further debate is needed on the shapes that machine awareness is likely to take. Although artificial neural networks are built on human brain connections, presuming that conscious artificial intelligence would naturally think and act in the same manner as humans do is a huge leap of logic. We don't know how machines think, and we need to investigate this. Remember the AI algorithms that had a discussion on social media that no one understood?

Humans could not comprehend it. So why not? We didn't comprehend how they were using language and, more significantly, we didn't grasp what incentives were driving the debate. Don't be afraid; embrace it.

A.I. is only a number.

You must comprehend that artificial intelligence is just a probability matrix of what should and should not be picked. Many people believe that when this scenario becomes a reality, robots would murder everyone and dominate the planet, but the fact is that even the most complicated robots on the market today are incapable of thinking for themselves. The rules that are in place inside their systems are developed by programmers, which means that they are predictable rules.

All of this is just scaled-up mathematics placed into machines to allow them to do the tasks that we need of them. Knowing that this is something that the typical person can perform, you should not be afraid of it. You should understand that practically of robotics developers throughout the globe do not have the intention of creating robots that are meant to remove people. People cannot get wealthy off of them, and any effort to do so would result in a worldwide uproar against the first person to do it. Essentially, it is one of those things that the whole world would condemn, and then we would have a slew of regulations making it harder for someone else to commit it.

Furthermore, creating anything like the Terminator is incredibly tough. You must understand that these robots can only function with soft bodies, and we are just now investigating how to manufacture such soft bodies. Because machines like the Terminator are substantially heavier, a turret within a robot is not physically possible. Rockets are impractical due to physics. Essentially, if you examine how the Terminator is created, you will rapidly discover that the Terminator that everyone fears is a physical impossibility as a weapon. That is feasible as an artificial intelligence stronger than most mankind. However, having a weapon armament contained inside the body is impossible if the robot reaches the size of a human. People are fragile constructs at best, incapable of sustaining a center of gravity. In reality, this is why creating a human-like machine is so difficult; the physics required for humanoid anatomy is incredibly tough to grasp. You could see something like MechWarrior that has such intelligence, but you are unlikely to see a robot that looks like a person and suddenly bursts out of a rocket. This is reality, and reality is founded on statistics; looking at the data, it is incredibly impossible to believe that robots would take over in the same manner that Terminator did. There's just so much wrong with the fundamental idea that it wouldn't operate in our environment. Don't allow the fear of a robot apocalypse to dictate how you use machine learning and artificial intelligence in your everyday life.

There are millions of ways for the world to end, and the robot apocalypse is simply one of them.

Decisions are made quickly.

It makes no difference whether you work in the healthcare business, the stock market, real estate, or any other profession that requires decision-making. Because robots can make judgments far quicker than people, they can affect a much larger shift in society. They can swiftly determine how to create more money, how to keep people safer, and overall decide things that benefit humanity quicker than humanity can decide by itself. Let's look at an example.

Assume that a vehicle will fall if it falls off one of the building's sides.

However, once the automobile begins moving, it cannot be stopped. A person would have a few seconds in which they would not make any decisions, and it would take them a few seconds to comprehend all that needed to be chosen. A computer, on the other hand, would be able to look at the scenario and determine what to do in nanoseconds after learning the rules. Machines can make decisions considerably quicker than humans and provide better results at a faster pace than humans can.

Don't allow large corporations to dictate your destiny if you can put your foot forward with little constraints on what you want to achieve.

Less Repetitive Work for Everyone

No one enjoys performing repeated work unless it is something that is not considered a repetitive job but rather a sort of leisure. For example, although many people like fishing, it is a vocation performed by just a few individuals; otherwise, Red Lobster would not exist. It is not considered a job unless the details are discussed.

Artificial intelligence enables us to automate the tedious tasks that most people despise. No one wants to concentrate on driving for 5 hours at a time, no one wants to pick vegetables from 100 acres, and no one wants to guarantee the cleanliness of the sewers themselves, all of which can be performed by artificial intelligence. Don't let the worry that no one will be able to find a job prevent you from inventing and enabling individuals to choose occupations that they are more interested in. You may choose whether there will be a shortage of employment or if the jobs that are offered will be occupations that people like performing.

Will Humans and Artificial Intelligence Coexist in the Future?

It is natural in nature for species to develop together or for particular species to adapt to changes in other species. So, we witness insects and tiny animals evolve camouflage to avoid predators, but then we see predators change their hunting schedules or weaponry to better capture their disguised prey. We observe giant predators like lions hunt in groups to overwhelm their massive bovine food, but we also see prey develop to move in packs to avoid assault by those that prey on them. This form of waltz, or coevolutionary dance, is ubiquitous in nature and contributes to the natural equilibrium that exists among Earth's species. Humans and technology may both advance in a coevolutionary dance, for better or worse. As IoT and smartphone usage have grown more common, parents are increasingly equipping their young children with this technology, which implies that these children will grow up to be people who are proficient at dealing with tech and AI and have expectations about IoT that differ from their parent's expectations.

It would be weird for these young people to work in offices where, for example, artificial intelligence (AI) was sold to clients but not employed by the company to address its own issues.

As the public changes to meet technological breakthroughs originating in business, firms must also adapt to meet the public's expectations. This adds another layer to this coevolution (the evolution of the public and the development of business as independent entities), and it only helps to further embed technology like AI in society. What this means, in the long run, is that AI will become truly ubiquitous one day, and the businesses that keep close tabs not only on AI developments, but also on how their own AI behaves, will be the most successful, as they will be able to handle the inevitable learning errors, predictive analysis missteps, and other AI problems. Just as it is prudent for a government to attempt to forecast social issues and fix them before they exist, corporations may attempt to predict and solve AI difficulties.

While many of us may be unaware that artificial intelligence is present in so many aspects of our life today, it has been widely acknowledged. Many various sorts of programs and devices already employ this technology--or at least a subset of artificial intelligence--to help them operate, and we use them without even thinking about it in our everyday lives.

True, when most people hear about artificial intelligence, they believe it is something far out of reach, something only those who have worked in the field of technology can understand. However, if you have ever worked on a search engine, had advertising appear on one of the websites you were browsing or used voice recognition software such as

Alexa, you have already had some experience with artificial intelligence in action.

We may not believe that we will embrace AI or that we will ever utilize it in our daily lives, but you most certainly have, and it will continue to expand. This is not at all a terrible thing. Accepting AI and incorporating it into various aspects of our life on a daily basis may benefit everyone involved. It can make your life simpler; it can help us explore new technologies, it can help companies succeed, and it can help us accomplish our jobs so much better than before.

Many of us may not comprehend or recognize when artificial intelligence is being employed in our lives, yet it is there and vital. Many chores are now considered commonplace in our lives, and the systems behind these acts will be managed by artificial intelligence. The fact that we were unaware of the technology and were performing all of the labor does not diminish its significance.

And when we begin to see all of the locations where this artificial intelligence may appear, you will become more receptive and open to employing this kind of technology as well.

Let us look at some of the easy everyday ways that AI is already being accepted in our culture, even if we aren't aware of it. These are not the only instances of how machine learning and artificial intelligence are being utilized, but they are excellent examples that will help us understand where this kind of technology is at the moment and how it directly impacts us.

First and foremost, have you ever dealt with a talkable device? One to which you may ask a question or provide a command and it will answer.

This might be done on your phone by asking a question to perform a search or get directions, or it could be done on a TV or a device like Alexa. All of these are being conducted with the assistance of machine learning, which is a subset of artificial intelligence.

The machine learning on this site works because it assists the computer in recognizing your speech patterns and what you are saying to others. There's no way a coder could go in and figure out all of the words and demands you make ahead of time, much alone all of the numerous word options, dialects, and even languages. As a result, we use machine learning so that the software may begin to learn as it goes, becoming more adept at determining what the user wants.

This is why, at first, it may seem that the object is having difficulty understanding what you are saying, and there are generally a few bumps in the road. However, if you've owned the gadget for a while and have worked with it, it gets a lot simpler. You will be able to make requests and ask queries without any difficulty.

Another example is when you do a search query on your preferred search engine. We've all spent time searching the internet for information, looking for a phone number, asking a question, and so on. And we all have certain preferred search engines that we utilize on a regular basis.

These search engines, too, are built on the concept of machine learning. It can keep track of your inquiries and the results you choose along the way. It will then provide recommendations based on that information. The more time you spend with a certain search engine, the better the results will be for what you are searching for. This is because the search engine's algorithm is designed to learn your preferences as you use it.

This may also be seen at work when you visit a website or even your social media accounts and notice that unique adverts are depending on some of the websites you have previously visited and some of your interests. We've all visited a website and seen the adverts on the side and top of the page. Those are there to assist the person who operates the website or blog to earn money, but marketers can now target them to you precisely, making it simpler than ever to convince you to click on it and make a purchase.

This is why the adverts on your page seem to be more tailored to where you have been in the past and some of your interests.

The marketer wants to earn a profit from their efforts. If you are a man and they offer women's gowns, they do not want you to go to their advertising. You are unlikely to click it, wasting their time and money in the process.

We discovered that the adverts you see on these websites are better tailored to you and what you enjoy thanks to machine learning and some of the algorithms that come with it. You may not click on all of them, but when the advertisements are tailored to you and what you are most interested in, you are more likely to click and make a purchase, which is what advertisers and marketers hope for.

If you spend time on Amazon or other websites that make suggestions based on what you were seeing or purchasing in the past, this is also an indication of artificial intelligence. These firms use different algorithms to match you with other consumers who purchased comparable things or other products that are already similar to what you have purchased or at least what you have been looking through.

The objective with this one is that you will see the item, enjoy it, and buy it again. This will not attract every consumer, but many marketers understand that it is a terrific strategy to earn a little more on each customer and gain repeat customers, improving their bottom line.

Before the recommendation system becomes excellent at its job, it must first learn about the consumers' purchasing patterns, what they prefer to buy, and so on. However, it will improve with time, and the consumer will be more inclined to make another purchase.

These are only a few instances that you may face on a daily basis, but there are many more that you will most likely encounter without even realizing it. Have you ever had your bank place a hold on your card or notify you because they suspected fraud?

Whether or not someone else using your card (humans make errors), there was a fraud detection program in place that used artificial intelligence to keep your financial information protected.

Have you ever submitted a loan application? It is possible that a computer programmed with artificial intelligence, rather than merely a loan officer, reviewed your application to determine whether it met their requirements.

The loan officer would go through and double-check items to ensure that everything matched the standards, but the smart machine would be able to go over them quickly ahead of time, saving the loan officer time and labor. It is feasible that when you are denied a loan, you are being rejected by an artificial intelligence-driven system rather than another person.

Even our airline tickets might vary in price. Some of the larger airlines will use an algorithm that will boost ticket costs on the busiest days and drop them on less-busy days. This is why the prices we pay for airline tickets vary so much depending on when we buy them and where we want to go for our vacation.

Machine learning and artificial intelligence are newer concepts that we are currently learning about and may not know much about just now. But it doesn't mean there isn't a lot of potentials here that we might use for our own purposes. And we can see from all of the cool innovations that come with machine learning and artificial intelligence that many individuals in society have already adapted and accepted this kind of technology. With the passage of time, this acceptability will probably rise as well.

As you can see, machine learning and artificial intelligence appear in your everyday life in a variety of ways, even if you were unaware of their presence, to begin with. This kind of technology is beginning to take over and, slowly but steadily, it is taking on new tasks that assist to make our lives simpler in general. And, undoubtedly, as time passes, this kind of technology will continue to advance, and we will begin to see more artificial intelligence seep into our lives.

Conclusion

As artificial intelligence takes on a larger role in contemporary culture, businesses must either keep up with AI breakthroughs or risk being overtaken by firms that are better at adapting. When dealing with businesses, both workers and members of the public will anticipate certain parts of AI, such as natural language processing and picture recognition, not to mention the virtual assistants and customer service AI that are becoming more widespread. This results in the coevolution of humans and technology, and just as species that fail to develop are washed away in nature, companies that fail to adapt will face the same destiny.

There is no excuse for organizations and their executives to fail in this area when adapting to a changing business environment is as easy as adopting AI into your firm. Even the most inexperienced individual may see the advantages of artificial intelligence. These advantages include the automation of processes that AI is likely to perform more efficiently and quickly than humans, the augmentation of processes with AI that is capable of engaging in multiple complex tasks with data due to machine learning, and machine learning itself, which allows AI to learn from the information that it has been exposed to.

Many business leaders (and others interested in artificial intelligence) find themselves in the sometimes-difficult position of needing to incorporate AI into their enterprise strategy without having a technical background in computer science or data science that would allow them to gain a thorough understanding of this technology. Indeed, a survey of AI research, or simply a reading of journals that keep up with AI breakthroughs, often entails or forays into extremely technical areas that may easily befuddle someone with no training in this sort of scientific discipline.

Fortunately, artificial intelligence problems are simply data questions, and organizations can always start there. Hopefully, company executives, especially C-suite members, and those interested in learning about AI will have a better knowledge of the kind of data measurements that are crucial in their operations. Crop yields, machine operating data, water data, and varied schedules may all be essential business information types in agriculture that are vital to the operation and the AI. In its most basic form, AI may be used to automate agricultural activities or to monitor different elements of a business.

As a result, artificial intelligence has immense potential in the field of business intelligence. company intelligence, or the study of information vital to company operations, is gaining relevance alongside AI. This, in and of itself, is a kind of coevolution. Appropriate usage of artificial intelligence necessitates that firms have a better grasp of their data and develop methods to make it more accessible to both AI and employees. This implies that in today's more technological and competitive business environment, firms are being forced to look at artificial intelligence in ways they may not have previously.

When it comes to adapting to AI, large technology corporations serve as models for smaller enterprises to emulate. These companies have been active in two major elements of AI that are essential to businesses: corporate AI strategy and the development of AI products that can be marketed to customers. As much as small companies may believe they are at a disadvantage when it comes to AI innovation, smaller organizations are able to carve a path for themselves in a business environment that allows for both big and small firms.

There is no doubt that large tech operations have the financial and human resources to be leaders in AI in ways that smaller companies may find difficult, but because of aspects of AI such as IoT, even smaller companies can see profits and assume prominent roles as innovators. The Internet of Things, or IoT, has played a significant role in the AI revolution since it symbolizes the vector that AI employs to fulfill its responsibilities. As more gadgets connect to the internet and people gravitate toward smart home and smart city technologies, there may be possibilities for organizations of all sizes simply because of the sheer number of AI iterations that will be accessible in the future.

Indeed, this final point is both an essential trend in AI and an enterprise strategy that organizations should consider. Artificial intelligence is most potent when it is given the opportunity to perform various jobs rather than being constrained by simple, supervised learning techniques that effectively restrict AI's predictive capabilities. AI agents will be engaged in multifactorial activities in the future, including a range of data inputs and outputs, as well as the building of sophisticated and diverse mathematical models. Because this marks a degree of innovation beyond where many organizations are now, it is in the best interests of enterprises to join the AI world today rather than waste time catching up.

Indeed, this is one of the most critical reasons why organizations and their executives should address AI concerns now rather than later. AI development is unlikely to halt. Businesses that do not adopt AI today will face an uphill battle that might lead to company loss. A company that is compelled to play catch-up is unlikely to ever succeed in doing so. AI issues such as investing in skilled employees and utilizing AI as a tool to enhance communication between leadership and employees are not only byproducts of AI technology adoption but are fundamentally positive improvements to the organization.

Much time has been spent in this book arguing for skilled employees as an essential form of company resource. Artificial intelligence technology is not yet at the stage where it can operate autonomously with moral or even entirely accurate conduct. As we've shown, even picture-labeling software may be troublesome. Although AI is expected to replace certain employees in many firms, it will also increase the importance of staff people who are versed in this sort of technology. The major tech corporations all have highly skilled machine learning teams, and smaller enterprises may profit from jumping on this industry trend.

Developing a thorough grasp of your data is just as crucial as recruiting people. Data is the money that AI uses in order to learn and execute analytical procedures. Businesses must consider what data points are relevant to them, where the data is housed, who is looking at the data, and how the data is linked with AI. These are basic fundamental business intelligence queries that illustrate operations adopting AI capabilities into their BI.

Businesses' ability to innovate and prosper in an increasingly competitive business environment will need a grasp of artificial intelligence - both its nomenclature and the trends that will influence it in the future. A C-suite that understands these components of AI will be better able to exploit the insights generated from AI, make better business choices, and engage more effectively with highly critical tech workers, such as computer scientists and data scientists. In many aspects, artificial intelligence is likely to democratize companies (and data), but grasping what that means requires first going on the thrilling artificial intelligence adventure.

9 783988 313683